CULTURE SMART!
SRI LANKA

Emma Boyle

First published in Great Britain 2009
by Kuperard, an imprint of Bravo Ltd
59 Hutton Grove, London N12 8DS
Tel: +44 (0) 20 8446 2440   Fax: +44 (0) 20 8446 2441
www.culturesmartguides.com
Inquiries: sales@kuperard.co.uk

Culture Smart! is a registered trademark of Bravo Ltd

Distributed in the United States and Canada
by Random House Distribution Services
1745 Broadway, New York, NY 10019
Tel: +1 (212) 572-2844   Fax: +1 (212) 572-4961
Inquiries: csorders@randomhouse.com

Series Editor Geoffrey Chesler
Design Bobby Birchall

ISBN 978 1 85733 476 0

British Library Cataloguing in Publication Data
A CIP catalogue entry for this book is available from the
British Library

Printed in Malaysia

Cover image: Painting from the Temple of the Tooth in Kandy. © Shanin/
Dreamstime.com
Images on pages 13, 54, 96, 103, 111, and 118 by courtesy of the author.
Images on the following pages by courtesy of Sri Lanka Tourism: 68, 131; 108 and
164 © Photego.co.uk; 113 © Martin Sewell
Images on pages 15 © André Perron; 16 © Irengarasu; 20, 22, 51 and 106 © Lankapic; 35
© Indi Samarajiva/Deshan Tennekoon; 39 © Ulflarsen; 70 © Kamala Lakshminarayanan;
72 © chikuado; 84 © Fotolia; 87 and 98 © iStockphoto.com; 101 and 123 © Anjadora;
102 © Soman; 109 © Morgendorfferr; 112 and 122 © Steve Evans; 121 © AlMare; 124
and 139 © Bernard Gagnon; 126 © Krankman; 133 © Antonious; 135 © Sarvodaya
Shramadana; 157 top © Marco Jansen; and 157 bottom © Symphoney Symphony.

About the Author

EMMA BOYLE is a British journalist and photographer who has lived in Sri Lanka since 2003. After graduating from Liverpool University in Philosophy and Politics she took a year out to travel, during which time she wrote for a variety of publications as she made her way around the world. Sri Lanka was the last stop on her journey, and it was to this country that she came back to pursue her passions of writing and photography. Emma now lives on the south coast of Sri Lanka with her Sri Lankan partner. She continues to contribute travel-related articles to a range of national and international magazines, publications, and newspapers, which have included *The Sunday Times* travel magazine and the Sri Lankan and Emirates in-flight magazines, and provides brochure and Web copy for the international travel company In Style.

The Culture Smart! series is continuing to expand.
For further information and latest titles visit
www.culturesmartguides.com

The publishers would like to thank **CultureSmart!**Consulting for its help in researching and developing the concept for this series.

CultureSmart!Consulting creates tailor-made seminars and consultancy programs to meet a wide range of corporate, public-sector, and individual needs. Whether delivering courses on multicultural team building in the USA, preparing Chinese engineers for a posting in Europe, training call-center staff in India, or raising the awareness of police forces to the needs of diverse ethnic communities, it provides essential, practical, and powerful skills worldwide to an increasingly international workforce.

For details, visit www.culturesmartconsulting.com

CultureSmart!Consulting and **CultureSmart!** guides have both contributed to and featured regularly in the weekly travel program "Fast Track" on BBC World TV.

contents

contents

Map of Sri Lanka

introduction

The pearl of the Indian Ocean; the land of
serendipity; Taprobane: Sri Lanka has been
known by various evocative names over the
centuries, and has been fought over and freed
from many an invasive power intent on
controlling the island's rich natural resources and
advantageous geographical position. The
influences of foreign powers, especially European,
have enriched Sri Lankan culture and are ever
visible facets in both the physical aspects of the
country and the mentality of the people.

Sri Lanka is renowned for its golden beaches,
beautiful Buddhist temples, and excellent Ceylon
tea, but it is just as famous for a crushing civil war
that over the last thirty years has continued to
unnerve a nation already divided by religion,
ethnicity, and language. What prospective visitors
might not know is that the country continues to
function normally, despite the conflict in the
north; rather than fall victim to its destabilizing
presence Sri Lankans are resilient. They have
learned to live and work harmoniously alongside
one another away from the conflict zones and
recognize the value of each other's individuality.

While urban centers are characterized by
frantic development, multinational businesses,
and a competitive telecommunications market,
the country's pace of change has been severely
dampened by the civil war, to the extent that

many rural areas have remained ensconced in a much earlier period of Sri Lanka's history. Many ingrained cultural traditions, especially in the most rural areas, have had little influence from the outside world, resulting in their natural and effortless preservation.

Sri Lanka shares many attributes with its South Asian neighbors, but the fact of its having one of the highest literacy rates in the region has resulted in a politically conscious, interested, and engaging people who take great pride in their country. Sri Lankans are genuinely friendly, welcoming, and cheerful people who take great pleasure in hosting Westerners who respect their culture. Loyalty is highly valued, and relationships are considered more important than time or money.

Culture Smart! Sri Lanka outlines the country's diverse and complex history, and unearths the forces that have shaped its sensibility and development over the years. It considers the multiethnic character of the country, and by touching on every aspect of life explains how this has formed the values and attitudes of the people. Offering an insight into how Sri Lankans interact with each other, both at home and in the workplace, and relating what they like to do and where they like to go, this book will enrich your visit to the island. Whether you come for business or for pleasure, you are sure to have a meaningful and memorable stay.

Key Facts

Official Name	Democratic Socialist Republic of Sri Lanka	
Capital City	Colombo. Population 653,000 (2003 est.)	Legislative capital: Sri Jayewardenepura Kotte
Main Cities	Kandy, Matara, Galle	
Area	25,332 sq. miles (65,610 sq. km) Similar in area to West Virginia	
Climate	Tropical monsoon. October–March: northeast monsoon. May–September: southwest monsoon. Heavy rain showers interspersed with periods of sunshine	The Hill Country has year-round rainfall. Temps. vary with altitude.
Land Use	Three-quarters of pop. live in rural villages; many are farmers. Arable land 14%; permanent crops 15%; protected parks and reserves 14%; other 43%.	Produce incls. tea, rice, sugarcane, coconuts, spices, rubber, grains, pulses, and fish.
Currency	Sri Lankan Rupee (Rs) At time of writing US $1 = Rs 107; 1 GBP = Rs 212.	The rupee is made up of 100 cents. One lakh = 100,000 rupees. The highest note is Rs 2,000.
Population	21,228,773 (2008 est.)	
Ethnic Makeup	Sinhalese 74%; Sri Lankan Tamils 12%; Muslim 7.5%; Indian Tamils 5.5%; others (e.g. Veddah, Burgher, Malay) 1%	

Age Structure	0–14 years 24.1% 15–64 years 68% 65+ years 7.9%	
Religion	Buddhists 70% Hindus 15% Muslims 7% Christians 7% Other 1%	
Languages	Sinhala and Tamil are the official languages.	English is spoken by about 10% of the population.
Government	The seat of government is in Colombo. The Executive President, elected for a six-year term, appoints his deputy, the Prime Minister.	Unicameral parliament of 225 members. There are nine administrative districts.
Media	Both private and state owned. TV and radio programs are in Sinhala, Tamil, and English.	Commercial stations include satellite and cable. Newspapers are also trilingual.
Media: English Language	Newspapers include *The Mirror*, *The Island*, *The Nation*, and *The Daily News*. Also, *The Sunday Observer* and *The Sunday Times*	
Electricity	230 volts, 50 Hz	Plugs have two or three round prongs. A set of plug adaptors is useful.
Video/TV	PAL system	
Telephone	The country code for Sri Lanka is 94	To dial out: 00 + country code
Internet Domain	.lk	
Time Zone	GMT + 5.5 hours (winter), GMT + 4.5 hours (summer)	

chapter one

LAND & PEOPLE

GEOGRAPHY

Evocatively shaped like a teardrop, the island of Sri Lanka is situated in the Indian Ocean, just twenty miles off the southern tip of India. Separated to the west by the Gulf of Mannar and to the north by the Palk Strait, Sri Lanka's only connection to India is a broken chain of limestone islands known as Adam's Bridge. With a surface area of 25,332 square miles (65,610 sq. km), Sri Lanka is similar in area to West Virginia, slightly smaller than Ireland, and twice the size of Belgium. It has a scenic 833-mile (1,340-km) coastline, and the northeastern port of Trincomalee is one of the largest and safest natural harbors in the world.

Sri Lanka packs a surprising variety of natural attractions within its humble physical proportions, having rolling plains, mountains, plateaus, rivers, jungle, rain forests, lagoons, and coastline, and has two distinct zones based on rainfall: the tropical "wet zone" (southwest) and the extensive "dry zone" (north and east).

The island's topographical features can be placed into three categories distinguishable by elevation: the coastal belt, the plains, and the mountains of the

Central Highlands. While the general terrain is mostly low and flat, interspersed with rocky outcrops that reach no more than a thousand feet, the hills and mountain peaks of the south central province reach elevations of more than 6,500 feet (1,981 m). Although Pidurutalagala (8,278 ft, or 2,523 m) is Sri Lanka's highest mountain, Sri Pada, or Adam's Peak (7,356 ft, or 2,242 m), a popular pilgrimage spot, is much better known.

The majority of the island's rivers have their source in the Central Highlands (the "Hill Country") and flow in a radial pattern toward the sea. Only sixteen rivers are more than 60 miles (97 km) long; at 208 miles (335 km) the Mahaweli Ganga is the longest. In the north, east, and southeast the (often seasonal) rivers feed numerous artificial lakes, ancient tanks, or reservoirs, which store water during the dry season. The flow of some of the larger rivers has been artificially controlled in order to create hydroelectric, irrigation, and transportation projects.

CLIMATE

With monsoons occurring on opposite sides of the
island at opposing times of the year, and as a result
of the elevated altitudes of the Hill Country, Sri
Lanka's climate is quite complex. Its position close
to the equator means that the country enjoys a
consistently warm climate with temperatures in
the coastal and lowland regions averaging around
82–86°F (28–30°C) year-round. At times it feels
much hotter, especially in the southwest "wet
zone," since humidity levels can reach 90 percent.
In the hills the story is quite different, since with
altitude come lower temperatures; the daily
average in Nuwara Eliya, Sri Lanka's highest town,
is a fresher 64°F (17°C), while nights are often
cold enough for frost.

The months of May to September see the
southwest monsoon bring wind and moisture
from the Indian Ocean to drop heavy rain over
the southwest region of the country, while from
October to March the northeast monsoon hits the
east coast less severely. At this time occur frequent
thunderstorms and heavy rains interspersed with
sunshine that often results in flash flooding. The
Hill Country, although affected by the southwest
monsoon, typically sees a lot of rainfall year-
round. Sri Lanka's "dry zone," located to the east
and north of the island, sees far less rainfall—an
annual average of about 59 inches (1,500 mm),
compared to 98 inches (2,500 mm) in the wet
zone—and most of this occurs only during the
monsoon period.

THE PEOPLE

Sri Lanka has a population of more than 21 million,
approximately 25 percent of whom live in cities.
Most Sri Lankans belong to one of four ethnic
groups identified by their language, their religion,
or both: the Sinhalese, the Tamils, the Muslims, and
the Burghers. The Veddahs make up a tiny fraction
of the total population alongside Parsis
(Zoroastrians of Persian origin), Borahs (Muslim
businessmen), and more recent European settlers.

The Sinhalese

The Sinhalese speak Sinhala,
and comprise 74 percent of the
population. Almost entirely
bound together through their
common belief in Theravada
Buddhism, their language and
shared heritage set them apart
from their Tamil and Muslim
neighbors. Forming the
majority in most districts
throughout the island except in
the Tamil homeland of the
north and the east, the Sinhalese are most densely
concentrated in the south and west of the island.

The Tamils

While all Tamils are united by their common
language, they are divided into two very distinct
groups—the Sri Lankan Tamils and the Indian
Tamils. In addition, the two groups have further

distinctions based on caste and dialect as well as religion; while Hindus constitute the majority of both Sri Lankan and Indian Tamils, a substantial number of each group follow Christianity.

The Sri Lankan Tamils are descendants of Dravidian (South Indian) settlers of the kingdoms of Anuradhapura and Jaffna, who arrived as long ago as the third century BCE. They comprise around 12 percent of the total population and make up majorities in the northern and eastern regions of the island.

The Indian Tamils, also called Hill Country Tamils, are descendants of laborers brought over

by the British in the nineteenth century to work on the tea, coffee, and rubber estates. The Indian Tamils live mainly in the Central Hill Country, reflecting their strong relationship with the plantation industry, and comprise approximately 5.5 percent of the total population.

The Muslims
Forming the largest ethnic minority after the Tamils, the Muslims are followers of Islam, and preserve their own cultural heritage, having

distinct sites of worship and social circles. Most Muslims are descendants of Arabic traders who began to arrive in Sri Lanka in the eighth century, soon after the founding of Islam. While most speak a form of Tamil peppered with Arabic words, many Muslims also speak Sinhala and English fluently. Muslims make up 7.5 percent of the population, and, while not in the majority anywhere, they make up large minorities in the north and east.

The Malays are also Muslim. Originating in Southeast Asia, they are descendants of soldiers, prisoners, and political exiles brought from Malaysia to Sri Lanka by the Dutch administration. They often speak a unique dialect of Malay in their homes.

The Burghers
The Burghers are a distinct ethnic group characterized by their European ancestry. When the Portuguese and Dutch came to Sri Lanka, many settled and intermarried with the local Sinhalese. The children of these unions could not claim citizenship either from the European country of their father or from the country of their birth, and the term "Burgher"—from the Dutch word *Vrij Burgher*, meaning "free citizen"—was born.

As the most Westernized of the island's ethnic groups, Burghers typically speak English as their first language, and are mainly Christian. Most Burghers live in the cities—Colombo, Matara, and Galle—and can be identified by their recognizably European-sounding surnames, such as Jansz, Da Silva, and Peiris.

The Veddahs

Also called the Wanniya-laeto (forest dwellers), the
Veddahs are descendants of the original Neolithic
community in Sri Lanka that dates from at least
16,000 BCE. They are a matrilineal society living in
small settlements in the eastern highlands, and
while they maintain little contact with other Sri
Lankan ethnic groups, only very few have retained
authentic fragments of their ancient culture. The
Veddahs are characterized by their native dress and
a social hierarchy preserved by local chieftains.

A BRIEF HISTORY

While Sri Lanka's ancient past is characterized by
frequent invasions, records of the island's early
history are colored so much by legend that it is
often impossible to determine the true course of
events. Certainly, until Buddhism arrived in the
island under King Devanampiyatissa, accounts of
the island's early history are based more on the
myths and legends of the time than on verifiable
historical facts. However, the one defining fact that
can be separated from fiction is that Sri Lanka has,
since earliest times, been a multiethnic society.

Prehistory

It is thought that Sri Lanka may have been
inhabited as far back as 125,000 BCE. While
archaeological evidence of early settlement patterns
is slight, it is thought that the Veddahs are the only
modern survivors of these prehistoric people.

Traditionally hunter-gatherers who used simple stone tools to live off the island's rich natural bounty, Veddahs are believed to have existed on the island since 16,000 BCE, ten centuries before the proclaimed arrival of the Sinhalese and Tamils.

Prince Vijaya

Prince Vijaya and his Indo-Aryan contingent from Northern India are the legendary founders of the Sinhalese race, and their arrival prior to the Dravidian (South Indian) Tamils in the third century BCE has been the subject of much debate. According to the Mahavamsa, a Buddhist chronicle of the island's early history, Vijaya, exiled from his father's kingdom, landed on the west coast of Sri Lanka—about where Mannar is today—on the same day as the Buddha gained enlightenment in 483 BCE. The prince and his 700 followers came ashore and settled in the river valleys, where they were able to cultivate rice. Slowly they made their way, through ingenious feats of hydraulic engineering, to settle in the island's dry northern plains. The largest of the evolving settlements became known as Anuradhapura.

Anuradhapura (377 BCE–933 CE)

The kingdom of Anuradhapura was legendarily founded in 377 BCE by Pandukabhaya, the fourth king of the Vijaya dynasty; however, it is for the time of King Devanampiyatissa (300–260 BCE) that the early Anuradhapura period is most significant, since it saw the arrival in Sri Lanka of Buddhism.

According to the *Mahavamsa*, Mahinda, the son of the mighty Emperor Asoka of India, arrived in Sri Lanka in around 246 BCE with a contingent of Buddhist monks, who quickly converted the King and later the entire Sinhalese population to Buddhism.

Buddhism essentially gave the Sinhalese their national identity. Devanampiyatissa established the monastery of Mahavihara—the historic center of Theravada Buddhism—and united Buddhism with the political state. In the first century CE the development of written scriptures instituted the Sinhalese with a literary tradition while the arrival of the Buddha's tooth relic in 371 CE became not only a religious symbol but also a symbol of sovereignty, since it was believed that whoever was in possession of the relic had the right to rule the island. Over

a short period, Buddhism achieved a divine status that quickly came to be regarded as the highest expression of Sinhalese culture.

Dutugemunu (161–37 BCE)
Sri Lanka's close proximity to India made it a constant target of invasion. Successful attempts

would result in a handful of Tamil kings reaching the throne at Anuradhapura—the longest serving of whom was Elara, a general who arrived around 205 BCE and ruled the kingdom for forty-four years. During this period there were other settlements outside Anuradhapura ruled by minor kings and chiefs, the largest of which was Mahagama (modern Tissamaharama). From this kingdom came the famous warrior-prince-turned-Buddhist-king Dutugemunu (161-37 BCE), who made it his life's ambition to defeat Elara, eventually succeeding after a fifteen-year campaign. Having battled his way through each minor kingdom on his way to Anuradhapura, Dutugemunu united the whole of Sri Lanka for the first time.

Successive kings were unable to preserve the unity achieved by Dutugemunu, and long periods of instability, periods of Tamil rule, and Indian invasions were to shape the events to come. By the fifth century CE Tamil influence in Sinhalese affairs was growing, due to the increasing reliance that Sinhalese kings placed on recruiting Tamil mercenaries to support them in their own internal disputes. Hinduism in India was experiencing a revival, and a Tamil identity in Sri Lanka was beginning to emerge. In the end, it was the Chola—an ancient South Indian Tamil kingdom—that brought about the downfall of Anuradhapura when they sacked the city in 993 CE.

Polonnaruwa (933–1255 CE)

The Cholas made their capital at the strategically defensible Polonnaruwa, sixty-two miles (100 km) to

the southeast, and ruled the island from India for seventy-five years. Purely for symbolic reasons, the Sinhalese kings remained in Anuradhapura, however the frustration of repeated invasions eventually spurred Vijayabahu I (1070–1110 CE) to drive out the Cholas from Sri Lanka, capturing Polonnaruwa in the process. He reigned for forty years, and during this time succeeded in restoring many Buddhist temples and monasteries that had been neglected under the Chola rule.

Vijayabahu died without an heir, and government was unstable until the advent of Parakramabahu I (1153–86), one of the country's most famous kings. Ambitious, indulgent, and a great patron of Buddhism, he launched a naval expedition against the Pandyas (an ancient South Indian Tamil kingdom who had defeated the Cholas) and Burma, and left a legacy of construction in the capital and island-wide reservoir-building that seriously depleted the royal treasury.

After Parakramabahu's death, the throne passed to his Tamil brother-in-law Nissankamalla (1186–96), who reigned peacefully for a decade before disunity and invasion prevailed, culminating in the terrorizing regime of Magha (1215–55) from Kalinga (a republic of central-eastern India), whose nonchalant attitude toward the upkeep of the capital contributed to its falling into disrepair. Gradually the population began to abandon the city to move further south.

The Kingdom of Jaffna

Even before the days of Polonnaruwa had drawn to a close, a kingdom was already beginning to emerge in the north of the country. Successive invasions by prominent South Indian Tamil empires, such as the Chola, Pandya, and Pallava, since the third century BCE, had consistently brought Dravidian settlers and so weakened the Sinhalese kings that by the end of the thirteenth century they had retreated as far south as the Hill Country. By 1340 the Sinhalese monarchy split, causing two rival kings to establish themselves at Gampola and Dedigama.

As a result of the increasing fragmentation of the Sinhala kings, the Tamil kingdom of Jaffna in the north of the island flourished; Tamils seized control of the valuable pearl fisheries located in the Jaffna Peninsula, and established the town as an important center for the trade in elephants and spices. As waves of fresh migrants arrived, South Indian Hindu culture in Jaffna became firmly established.

This was to cause a division. As the Sinhalese retreated further south an ever widening gap separated the northern Tamil and southern Sinhalese settlements. This had severe cultural implications, since it effectively resulted in the creation of two distinct ethno-linguistic zones whose diverging cultures had different religions, influences, and traditions at their heart.

The Portuguese (1505–1658)
By 1400, there were three firmly established kingdoms on the island: the Tamil kingdom of Jaffna in the north, the Sinhalese kingdom of Kandy in the Central Highlands, and a new Sinhalese kingdom at Kotte, on the west coast of the island, near to present-day Colombo. Of the two Sinhalese kingdoms, it was Kotte—valued for its monopoly on the spice trade—that had emerged as the most powerful.

Recognizing the import of its spice—especially cinnamon—trade, the Sinhalese kings began to look toward foreign trade. So in 1505, when a Portuguese fleet was blown off course and landed on the west coast of Sri Lanka, it was warmly received by the King of Kotte, Parakramabahu IX (1484–1508), who invited the Portuguese to build a residence at Colombo for trading purposes. However, as the opportunity to exploit Sri Lanka's precious offerings to the outside world grew, it soon became clear that Portuguese intentions were based on self-interest rather than on shared ideals.

Initially, the Portuguese were not interested in territorial gain—they did not have the manpower to support it—so they maintained good relations with the kings of Kotte. As their demands grew, however, relations soured, resulting in intermittent fighting that would continue until the death of King Rajasimha I (1581–93), when the Portuguese successfully annexed Kotte.

The Jaffna kingdom had, from the outset, remained hostile to the Portuguese, especially on account of their dogged determination to convert the Tamil Hindu population to Roman Catholicism. Despite King Kankili's (1616–19) furious massacre of the missionaries and their converts, Jaffna finally fell to the Portuguese in 1619. Only the independent kingdom of Kandy, which had aligned itself with the incoming Dutch, remained out of Portuguese reach.

The Dutch (1656–1798)
While the Portuguese were exploiting Sri Lanka's lucrative spice trade, the Dutch, already a dominating force in South Asia, were scheming to wrest control of this vital trade for themselves. They caught the attention of the Kandyan King Rajasimha II (1635–87), who saw them as a means of ridding the island of the Portuguese. In 1638 an agreement was signed that gave the Dutch a monopoly on the island's major trade goods in exchange for Sri Lankan autonomy.

As the Dutch set to work on expelling the Portuguese, it soon became obvious that they were not intent on honoring their original agreement. While the eastern ports of Trincomalee and Batticaloa, captured in 1639, were handed back to the Sinhalese, the Dutch refused to hand over the strategic western ports of

Galle and Negombo when they captured them the year after, thereby taking control of the island's richest spice lands. When the Portuguese finally surrendered Colombo to the Dutch in 1656 and Jaffna in 1658, Holland had gained control of all of the island's coastal regions. The Dutch then landlocked Kandy so that it would be unable to ally itself with another foreign power.

Having seized political control of the island, the Dutch concentrated mainly on the monopolization of trade, not only in spices but also in elephants, pearls, and betel nuts. Although efforts were made to enforce the Reformed Calvinist faith on the population (declaring Roman Catholicism illegal), the Dutch were far more tolerant of indigenous religions than the Portuguese.

The British (1796–1948)

The French Revolution (1789–99) caused unlikely
new relationships to be formed between leading
European powers. As a result, the Dutch permitted
the British—who had been eyeing the strategic
location of Trincomalee's harbor—entry to land in
Sri Lanka in 1796 on condition that they would
prevent it from falling into the hands of the French
Republicans. A further unspoken condition was
that the British would eventually hand back control
of the island to the Dutch. But this was not to be.
Under the 1802 Treaty of Amiens, the Dutch part
of the island became the Crown Colony of Ceylon.

By 1815, the British had also taken control of
the inland kingdom of Kandy, becoming the first
European power to do so, and the first rulers since
Nissankamalla to bring the whole country under
the control of a single power. Ironically, since the
Kandyan kingdom had maintained its
independence for so long, it was not by battle that
the British took the city but as a result of disunity
between disgruntled courtiers and their king, Sri
Wickrama Rajasinha (1798–1815). As a result of
Rajasinha's brutal suppression of the numerous
conspiracies against him, courtiers and residents
simply stood aside to let the British pass.

English became the official language of
government and, in order to open up the economy,
all state monopolies were abolished. In 1832
changes in property laws made it easier for British
settlers to buy land. This, combined with the sale of

Crown lands, resulted in plantations springing up everywhere. While the British were initially

interested in Sri Lanka only for her strategic naval importance, it soon became obvious that the creation and trade of the island's own products could be of vital economic import too. Coffee flourished, and from the 1830s to the 1870s there was a switch from the traditional reliance on subsistence crops to plantation agriculture. As a result, capital was quick to flow in.

In 1869 a devastating leaf blight was discovered, which destroyed almost all of the island's coffee crop within the next fifteen years. Fortunately, earlier experiments had shown that tea was well suited to the climes of the Hill Country and was soon to prove a more than adequate replacement. Rubber and coconut plantations were also flourishing. Since the British were unable to persuade the Sinhalese to work on the plantations, they imported a great number of Tamil workers as indentured laborers from South India, many of whose descendants continue to work on the plantations to this day.

The growth in the plantation industry paved the way for increased unity in the country, by way of the construction of roads linking the Hill Country plantations with the coastal ports. Railways were also established under the British and, along with hospitals, hydroelectric projects, and organized agricultural plantations, they provided the infrastructure for a viable national economy able to support its growing population.

The Rise of Nationalism

A revival of Buddhist and Hindu movements by individuals keen to preserve their culture in the face of repressive colonial rule was gaining strength by the late nineteenth century. Prominent figures such as the Buddhist activist Angarika Dharmapala and the American theosophist Henry Steel Olcott—a Buddhist convert—helped to politicize the movement. In 1910, the declaration that a small electorate of Sri Lankans was permitted to send one member to the Legislative Council marked a minor victory, which, combined with the spread of US-led national determinism in the interwar years, was to set the ball rolling toward further change.

In 1919 the Ceylon National Council was formed to campaign for self-rule, and, as the movement grew larger and more organized, relentless lobbying by united Sinhalese and Tamil organizations over the interwar years for constitutional reform finally paid off. In 1931 the introduction of universal suffrage for an elective legislature and an executive council, in which power was shared with the British, gave the island's leaders the chance to gain political power with a view toward eventual self-governance.

The independence movement had two streams—"constitutionalists" and radicals, who, following the Indian example, sought outright independence. During the Second World War the

mainstream Sinhalese leadership collaborated
closely with Britain, and Ceylon became Britain's
front-line base against the Japanese.

Independence

In February 1948, Sri Lanka gained independence
from Britain as "Ceylon," a dominion within the
British Commonwealth. The first independent
government was formed by the United
National Party (UNP)—an essentially
conservative coalition that represented
the island's major ethnic groups
bound by the common ideals of Sri
Lankan nationalism—under the
leadership of Don Stephen
Senanayake. For the first few years
everything looked good: exports were
doing well in world markets, the government had a
significant majority in parliament, and there was
little or no social unrest.

By the early 1950s, however, the situation had
changed. Falling rubber and tea prices on the
world market combined with high import prices
resulted in increasing economic difficulties. The
plantation Tamils suddenly found themselves
disenfranchised by the UNP—an event that
revealed for the first time serious fissures in the
body politic based on a Sinhalese and Tamil
ethnic divide. In 1951, the prominent nationalist
S. W. R. D. Bandaranaike led his faction, the
Sinhala Maha Sabha, out of the UNP to establish
the Sri Lanka Freedom Party (SLFP).

The Bandaranaike Era

Since the 1956 general election coincided with the 2,500th anniversary of the Buddha's enlightenment and of the legendary arrival of the Sinhalese Prince Vijaya, the SLFP, under Bandaranaike's leadership, swept to victory on largely nationalistic grounds. The new government quickly passed the Sinhala Only law, which, followed by the instigation of state support for Sinhalese–Buddhist culture, was to have lasting implications on a Tamil minority that was feeling increasingly threatened by the majority ethnic group. The growing tension would become politicized and lay the foundations for the future Sinhalese–Tamil difficulties that continue to dominate Sri Lanka today.

While the Bandaranaike government focused on policies of expanding the public sector and broadening domestic welfare, schemes restricting foreign investment and nationalizing critical industries and plantation land resulted in an inevitable slump in the economy and a growing feeling of discontent. When Bandaranaike was attempting in 1959 to bridge the growing ethnic divide by negotiating with Tamil leaders for a federalist solution he was assassinated by a militant Buddhist monk.

In the 1960 general election, the SLFP, under the leadership of Bandaranaike's widow, Sirimavo, swept to victory. Mrs. Bandaranaike, as she became known, became the world's first female prime minister. She continued broadly to follow her husband's policy of nationalizing key industries such as oil, while brutally enforcing the Sinhala Only law and deporting up to a million plantation Tamils back to India. Inevitably, ethnic tensions surfaced, and when riots broke out in the north and the east of the country she responded by curtailing Tamil political activity.

As discontent under the SLFP grew, the UNP triumphed in the 1965 general election. Declaring the economy to be virtually bankrupt, they attempted to create a mixed economy with an emphasis on the private sector, but with little success. By 1970 Mrs. Bandaranaike, head of a new SLFP coalition called the United Front, was elected back into government.

The Emergence of the JVP

The early 1970s saw the rise of the Sinhalese-Marxist anti-Tamil People's Liberation Army (Janatha Vimukthi Peramuna, or JVP), led by Rohana Wijeweera. Its members were largely students and young men impatient for radical change and united in frustration at the lack of employment opportunities available to the growing populace. In 1971, as the JVP attempted to overthrow the Bandaranaike government, serious fighting broke out in central and southern rural districts and left many dead. The military quickly moved to suppress the movement and imprison its leaders as well as thousands of suspected insurgents.

This widespread unrest allowed the government to call for wider controls. In 1972 the constitution changed the country's name from

Ceylon to the Democratic Socialist Republic of Sri Lanka. However, in the light of a declining economy and still rising

unemployment the SLFP were resoundingly defeated by the UNP in the 1977 general election.

J. R. Jayawardene

Under the leadership of J. R. Jayawardene, the UNP reversed the Bandaranaikes' statist policies and established an open economy actively looking to attract back foreign investment. Initially, these policies showed some success: unemployment was halved by 1983, the country became virtually self-sufficient in rice by 1985, while tourism and expatriate Sri Lankans living abroad brought in an increasingly good supply of foreign exchange, especially in the face of growing inflation and unstable tea and rubber prices.

In 1978 Jayawardene introduced a new constitution, which handed over executive power to the president—a role that had previously been largely ceremonial. Resigning from his post as prime minister, Jayawardene became president in that same year and, after a few tweaks to the constitution, was reelected by popular vote in 1982.

While relations between the Sinhalese and Tamils had declined since the 1950s, Tamil unrest had grown to irrecoverable proportions by the mid-1970s due in most part to their increasing alienation by the government; in legislation passed

in 1971, the number of places available to Tamils
in universities was cut while a constitutional law
decreed that Buddhism held the "foremost place"
in Sri Lankan culture. Although Jayawardene's
government made the concession of promoting
Tamil as the "national language" of business in
Tamil areas, this came too late.

As the Tamil movement became increasingly
politicized, so it also became violent as Tamil
militant groups began to form. In 1976, a group
of young people under the leadership of Velupillai
Prabhakaran established the Liberation Tigers of
Tamil Eelam (LTTE, or Tamil Tigers), which
would become one of the deadliest terrorist
groups in the world. They fought for a separatist
state in the north and east of the island that they
called Eelam.

Outbreak of Civil War

In 1983, growing tensions finally exploded. Tamil
Tiger guerrillas ambushed and killed an army
patrol in the Jaffna region, resulting in what was
later to be dubbed Black July. In the week following
the ambush Sinhalese mobs looted and killed
Tamils island-wide, virtually leveling areas with
large Tamil populations. It is not clear how many
Tamils died in the atrocities; estimates vary
between 400 and 3,000.

The fact that the government and security
forces seemed unable to put a stop to the violence
led many Tamils to flee overseas. Violence
continued to erupt between the two sides and by

1985, despite the government's belated offer of limited Tamil self-government, security forces and the LTTE were engaged in skirmishes in the north and down the east coast. As a result, the country's economy took a nosedive as tourism slumped, foreign investment dried up, and military spending soared.

The Indian Peace Keeping Force

By 1987, government forces had isolated the LTTE in Jaffna City. Hoping to calm the situation, they had also signed an accord to create new councils for Tamil areas in the north and east. However, as fighting continued and thousands of displaced Tamils fled to the relative safety of Tamil Nadu's refugee camps in India, Jayawardene struck a deal with the Indian president, Rajiv Gandhi, to replace government troops with an Indian Peace Keeping Force (IPKF). By doing this, it was hoped to encourage the LTTE rebels to disarm and therefore return the north and the east of the country to peace.

In a short time it became apparent that this deal suited no one. While the LTTE was quiet for a time, frequent clashes with the IPKF soon resulted in an escalation into war. The LTTE was not the only group to oppose the deal; the Muslim quarter and the Sangha (community of Buddhist monks) voiced their disagreement, while Sinhalese nationalists—enraged that there was a foreign army on Sri Lankan soil—demanded that the IPKF leave. Although successful in containing the LTTE for a time, the IPKF left in March 1990.

Return of the JVP

In 1987, as another wave of Sinhalese nationalism was ignited by the presence of the IPKF, the left-wing JVP exploited the opportunity to make a comeback. Inspired by communism and impatient for radical change, it proved to be more organized and more deadly than before. Still led by Rohana Wijeweera, it now included not only students and the unemployed but also monks, the police, and the army, which launched a series of attacks and political assassinations across the south and center that brought the terrified country virtually to a standstill.

In 1988, President Jayawardene was succeeded by a new UNP leader, Ramasinghe Premadasa, who defeated Mrs. Bandaranaike in the ensuing presidential election. As well as pledging to end the fighting with the LTTE in the north, Premadasa immediately implored the JVP to lay down their arms. When they refused he sent out paramilitary death squads designed to hunt down each and every member of the JVP leadership. By 1989 most of the higher-ranking JVP activists, including Rohana Wijeweera, had been killed or imprisoned, and the rebellion was extinguished. While it is estimated that tens of thousands of people were killed in the insurrection, the JVP soon became, and remains today, a main part of the political mainstream.

The 1990s

Not long after the IPKF withdrawal, hostilities between the LTTE and the Sri Lankan government resumed. Most probably in retaliation for his part in agreeing to Jayawardene's request to station the IPKF in Sri Lanka, Rajiv Gandhi was assassinated when an LTTE cadre member blew herself up in front of him on his campaign trail in Tamil Nadu in 1991. President Premadasa was also the victim of a suspected LTTE suicide bomber when he was killed at a May Day rally in 1993.

In 1994 the leftist People's Alliance (PA)—a coalition with the SLFP—won the parliamentary election, thus ending seventeen years of UNP rule. Its leader, Chandrika Bandaranaike Kumaratunga, the daughter of the former Bandaranaike prime ministers, became the country's first female president. Moving well away from the SLFP's traditionally nationalistic roots, Kumaratunga strove for economic liberalization and national reconciliation with the aim of ending the civil war.

Despite peace talks between the government and the LTTE soon after Kumaratunga's election, the conflict showed no signs of abating. As government forces continued to attack LTTE positions, winning Jaffna in 1995, the LTTE responded with more bombs, the most notable targets of which were the Central Bank in 1996, the Temple of the Tooth in Kandy in 1998, and the international airport in 2000. Just days before her successful presidential reelection in December 1999, Kumaratunga was also the target of a suicide bomber and narrowly escaped, with the loss of her sight in one eye. Despite her successful election for a second term, Kumaratunga seemed unable to move toward a lasting peace.

Cease-Fire

Parliamentary elections were again held in 2001, resulting in the victory of the UNP under the leadership of Ranil Wickramasinghe. Kumaratunga remained as president. As prime minister, Wickramasinghe quickly moved to open negotiations with the LTTE, finally bringing them to the negotiating table, assisted by Norwegian peace monitors, to sign a cease-fire declaration in February 2002. Events moved quickly thereafter: weapons were decommissioned; the A9 road joining the Jaffna Peninsula to the rest of the island was reopened after twelve years; passenger flights to Jaffna were resumed; and the government lifted the ban on the LTTE. Most importantly, the LTTE surrendered its demand for an independent state in favor of a federal system.

At the beginning, hopes for a lasting peace looked positive. By the end of the year, however, relations between Kumaratunga and Wickramasinghe had soured to the extent that disagreements over the implementation of the peace process—she believed the government was making too many concessions to the rebels—resulted in the LTTE's withdrawal from talks in April 2003. Later that year Kumaratunga used her powers to dissolve parliament (despite the UNP's having a mandate to govern until 2007) and call for an election. As a result of a new SLFP coalition with the JVP, Kumaratunga's Freedom Alliance (FA) narrowly achieved the majority it needed to defeat the UNP in the April 2004 parliamentary elections.

Meanwhile, the LTTE suffered setbacks of its own; many countries, including the USA, the UK, and later the EU, began listing the LTTE as a Foreign Terrorist Organization, while the LTTE's commander in the east, Colonel Karuna, broke away from the movement, taking several thousand troops with him. While Karuna fled underground, later to renounce terrorism and join the government as a member of parliament in 2008, the LTTE regained control of its eastern wing.

With the new prime minister, Mahinda Rajapakse, at the helm, the peace process stalled; violence in the east of the country between the LTTE, the Karuna faction, and the Sri Lanka military, combined with a suicide bomb in Colombo—the first since 2001— and the departure of the Norwegian mediators, undermined all confidence in the peace process. However, the economy, buoyed by high tourist numbers, continued to do well.

THE TSUNAMI

On December 26, 2004, an earthquake off the Indonesian coast triggered a tsunami that brought devastation to nearby countries. Sri Lanka suffered heavily. Three-quarters of its coast was reduced to rubble; more than 30,000 lives were lost; millions of people were displaced; thousands of buildings were destroyed; half of the island's fishing fleet was washed away; and vital sections of road and railway line disappeared. The economic loss was huge: estimated damage stood at well over US $1 billion. In the face of this great tragedy, it seemed that the nation's differences might finally be resolved. However, as people struggled to cope, the government and the LTTE became embroiled in an argument over distribution of aid in Tiger-controlled areas.

When a controversial US $3 billion aid-sharing agreement, which allowed the LTTE to distribute aid to displaced people in the north and east, was ratified by parliament in June 2005, President Kumaratunga was criticized by JVP colleagues and Buddhist monks. Fiercely opposed to this agreement, which they believed would establish the LTTE as a de facto government in the north, the JVP walked out of the FA coalition—thus depriving it of its parliamentary majority—and then successfully pressured the Supreme Court into suspending the agreement.

Mahinda Rajapakse

In the November 2005 presidential election, widely
thought to be one of the most crucial in Sri Lanka's
history, the prime minister, Mahinda Rajapakse,
narrowly triumphed over Ranil Wickramasinghe, the
peace-oriented UNP leader who had brokered the
original 2002 cease-fire. The election was boycotted
by the LTTE, which forced people in Tiger-controlled
areas not to vote. Although the LTTE's reasoning
behind the boycott was not clear, Wickramasinghe
was the preferred candidate of the minorities, so the
loss of a potential 180,000 votes probably cost him
the presidency.

When Rajapakse was sworn in
as president, he vowed to continue
peace talks with the LTTE.
However, supported by the JVP
and a party of Buddhist monks,
he rejected the idea of Tamil
autonomy and refused to share
tsunami aid, initiating a
confrontational anti-Tamil agenda.

As the first anniversary of the tsunami approached,
world leaders, aid agencies, and the global community
urged the government and the LTTE to end the
postelection upsurge in violence and return to peace
talks. Both parties agreed, and on February 22, 2006,
peace talks were resumed in Geneva. While
expectations were low, commitments to end the
violence were made on both sides. However, these
declarations lasted barely a month. By the end of
March the Sri Lankan Navy and the LTTE were in

conflict off the coast of Trincomalee. In April, when an LTTE suicide bomber in the main military compound in Colombo killed eight, the military launched air strikes on Tamil Tiger targets in the north, which forced tens of thousands of civilians to flee their homes. Further Sri Lankan Air force (SLA) attacks against LTTE targets in the north followed a mine attack on a crowded bus in Anuradhapura, which killed sixty-four civilians.

War had resumed in all but name as clashes, killings, bomb attacks, and fighting continued between the two sides throughout 2006. In October, as peace talks were set to resume in Geneva between the two sides, an LTTE suicide bomber killed over ninety sailors in a military convoy near Habarana. LTTE militants also attacked a naval base in Galle. As the Norwegian monitors continued to report repeated open violations of the truce by both the government and the Tamil Tiger rebels, it was clear that the cease-fire remained only in name.

March 2007 saw the Tamil Tigers reach new levels when they launched their first-ever air raid against a military base near the international airport. They followed this with another attack in July on an air force base in Anuradhapura, setting a new precedent in the long-running civil war. Hostilities continued to intensify, and by the end of the year the government had finally regained control of the Eastern Province.

In January 2008 the government announced its withdrawal from the 2002 cease-fire agreement with pledges to win the war within a year. Bomb attacks, political assassinations, disappearances, and heavy fighting in the north were to form the growing pattern of progress. In May elections were held to fill the newly created Eastern Provincial Council, which was won by the UPFA in coalition with the Tamil Makkal Viduthalai Pullikal (TMVP) party. The TMPV leader Sivanesethurai Chandrakanthan (otherwise known as Pillaiyan) was sworn in as Chief Minister.

GOVERNMENT AND POLITICS
Sri Lanka is a democratic government, with an executive president who is both head of state and head of government as well as Commander-in-Chief of the sizeable armed forces. While Sri Lanka gained independence from Britain in February 1948, the present constitution, which provides for an executive president based on the French model, was not adopted until August 1978. Despite the ongoing civil war with the LTTE, and the high levels of political violence associated with the JVP during the 1980s, the government is relatively stable. No military coups or uprisings have toppled it during its existence.

The terms of the 1978 Constitution state that Sri Lanka is a Democratic Socialist Republic. All citizens are equal before the law, and in recognition of the pluralistic character of Sri Lankan society, no discrimination should be made on grounds of ethnicity, religion, language, or caste. The legal voting age is eighteen, and there are two official languages: Sinhala and Tamil.

Sri Lanka has a multiparty system, which is dominated by the current ruling socialist Sri Lanka Freedom Party (SLFP) and the conservative United National Party (UNP). The politics of Sri Lanka reflects the historical differences between the two main ethnic groups.

Sri Lanka is divided into nine provinces, eight of which have councils with limited powers in the areas of education, health, rural development, social services, agriculture, and local taxation. Provincial councils are directly elected for a five-year term and the head of the council majority serves as chief minister. Beneath them are municipal, urban, and village councils.

The Executive
The president is involved in every aspect of government. Responsible to parliament for the exercise of duties under the constitution and laws, the president may be removed from office by a two-thirds majority in parliament with the agreement of the Supreme Court. The prime minister is appointed by the president from the ruling party, to be his deputy and head of cabinet.

In presidential elections, the winner must gain more than 50 percent of the public vote, and is qualified to serve a term of six years, which can be extended to a second term. The next presidential elections are due to take place in 2011.

The Legislature

Sri Lanka has a unicameral legislature, with 225 seats. Members are directly elected by a system of modified proportional representation for a period of six years. Although the president has the power to summon, suspend, or end a legislative session, parliament reserves the power to make and change all laws.

In 2004 the UPFA, a coalition of the People's Alliance (PA) and the Marxist Janatha Vimukthi Peramuna (JVP), gained 104 out of the 225 seats, falling short of a majority. In June 2005, the JVP left the coalition government, leaving the UPFA in a minority. However, since 2007 a number of UNP members have joined the government team, and in a new coalition with the Sri Lanka Muslim Congress (SLMC) and the TMVP the government has recently gained a parliamentary majority. The next elections are scheduled for 2010.

The Judiciary

The judiciary consists of the Supreme Court and the Court of Appeal, whose judges are appointed by the president, as well as a High Court and a number of subordinate courts. Independent of the executive and the legislature, Sri Lanka's legal system reflects both history and diverse cultural influences. While criminal law remains fundamentally British, basic civil law is Roman-Dutch. Kandyan, Jaffna, and Muslim laws still retain substantial regional influence in personal disputes.

Foreign Relations

Sri Lanka has traditionally followed an internationally nonaligned foreign policy, although it has sought closer relations with the USA since 2001. It participates in multilateral diplomacy, particularly in the UN, with aims to promote sovereignty, independence, and development in the developing world. Sri Lanka was a founding member of the Non Aligned Movement (NAM) and has remained a member of the Commonwealth since independence. It is also a member of the South Asian Association for Regional Co-operation (SAARC), the World Bank, the International Monetary Fund (IMF), and the Asian Development Bank (ADF).

THE ECONOMY

Historically, Sri Lanka's economy has been heavily dependent on agriculture. However, since the 1970s it has become highly diversified. Foreign investment has been encouraged, while the manufacturing and service sectors have rapidly overtaken agriculture in terms of GDP; although the agriculture still employs just over a third of Sri Lanka's 7.76-million-strong labor force, plantation crops as the main source of exports fell from 90 percent in the 1950s to just 16 percent in 2007, while the manufacturing sector, which was practically nonexistent fifty years ago, accounts for more than 60 percent of exports today.

Since 2004, under the ruling SLFP, agriculture has seen a revival as the government aims to support domestic enterprise and reduce poverty by steering investment to disadvantaged areas. However, an increase in government expenditure since 2006— caused by a rising defense budget and an expansion of an already huge civil service coupled with rising world oil prices—has resulted in rising inflation.

The government encourages the development of small- and medium-scale enterprises (SMEs), and while Sri Lanka has a mixed economy, the privatization of all state enterprises has presently been put on hold. Today, Sri Lanka's most dynamic areas are textiles, clothing, food, drink, port construction, telecommunications, insurance, and banking. The services sector, which includes income from tourism, is the largest sector of the economy; it employs 41 percent of the total labor force and contributes roughly 57 percent of GDP.

Exports are Sri Lanka's largest foreign exchange earners. Its biggest exports are clothing, tea, cut diamonds, and jewelry, coconut products, rubber, and fish. Major imports include textile fabrics, mineral products, petroleum, foodstuffs, machinery, and transportation equipment. The USA, India, UK, and China are Sri Lanka's largest trading partners. Sri Lanka also relies heavily on foreign aid and the remittances of the more than 800,000 Sri Lankans who live abroad and send home in excess of US $1 billion each year.

chapter two

VALUES & ATTITUDES

Sri Lanka shares many core values with other South Asian countries. Irrespective of religion or ethnicity, great importance is placed on the value of education; religion is a significant part of daily life; and family ties, tradition, and the community are held in high regard. Despite being divided by ethnicity, social background, and religion, Sri Lankans, in common with other former European colonies in Asia, are united through a shared pride in their national identity.

Sri Lanka, like much of South Asia, is a patriarchal society. However, as a result of the country's free educational system and the introduction of postindependence egalitarian social policies, women in Sri Lanka have more advantages than their South Asian sisters. Literacy is almost universal, and while traditional attitudes remain, especially in the more rural areas, there is greater equality between the sexes at home and in the workplace, especially in comparison to Sri Lanka's closest neighbor, India.

CASTE AND CLASS

Sri Lankans are very aware of social order and status. As a result of the traditional caste system, the idea of social equality remains a foreign concept to many Sri Lankans, even though it has seen national acceptance in the country's constitutional and legal framework. All relationships still involve hierarchies to some extent, although merit and achievement have begun to outweigh caste and class.

The caste system played an important role in the island's traditional rural society, where stratification occurred primarily as a result of the trade, craft, or profession a person was born into. While caste is hardly visible in society today, save for its influence in the marriage market, there remain some occasions within ethnic groups where subdivisions relating to caste or even racial descent occur. The Dutch Burghers see themselves as superior to the Portuguese Burghers, while among the Sinhalese the Kandyans claim superiority because their kingdom was the last to fall to the colonial powers. Caste is most evident among the Tamils, and although the hierarchy of each group differs slightly, the Jaffna Tamils believe theirs to be superior.

Although Sri Lanka's social structure traditionally consisted of the rulers and the ruled, the nineteenth century saw the rise of the Sri Lankan middle class. In the seventeenth century the Portuguese had enlisted and elevated those from other social groups in return for loyal service, thus creating the *Mudaliyar* caste, and it went on to flourish under the British colonial government. These Westernized, primarily urban professionals (lawyers, doctors, teachers, and skilled workers) competed with the traditional Sri Lankan elite to form a new class of achievers that transcended divisions of race and caste. When free education was introduced in 1944, followed by a focus on equality-based social welfare policies, it further became possible for achievers from all walks of life and of both sexes to transcend the class divide.

Sri Lankan society today is loosely split into three social groups: a small class of very wealthy urbanites, a growing middle class, further divided into an upper and lower level, and the rural poor. Sri Lankans typically socialize within their own groups (although exceptions occur), and there is an obvious division between the rich elite— identified by their command of English, education in exclusive schools, and expensive possessions—and the poor, nowhere more so than in Colombo, where wooden shacks sit alongside huge mansions. There are also further divisions based on the differing values of the urban and rural population.

RELIGION

Sri Lanka is multireligious; the majority, Buddhists, live peacefully beside sizeable Hindu, Muslim, and Christian communities, while major local events, such as the opening of a school, are often marked by representatives of each faith together. The value of religion to each ethnicity is equally important: they regularly practice their faith at home as part of the daily routine—lighting candles, praying—and try to live by its code of conduct. The festivities of each religion are woven deeply into the island's culture, and some pilgrimage sites are shared; Kataragama is venerated by Muslims, Buddhists, and Hindus alike, while the famous footprint atop Adam's Peak is worshipped by all.

Buddhism

Dating from the third century BCE, Sri Lanka was one of the first countries in the world to adopt Buddhism, and it has always played a significant spiritual, cultural, and at times political role in the country. Sri Lanka is the preserver of some of Buddhism's most important scriptures, since it was here that the Buddha's teachings were first committed to writing in 30 BCE. Much of Sri Lanka's culture, in the form of painting, sculpture, and literature, is inspired by Buddhist ideals.

Theravada Buddhism—the embodiment of the Buddha's teachings, or *dharma,* in Pali (the ancient language of India derived from

Sanskrit)—is most commonly practiced in Sri Lanka. The Buddha emphasized that each person is responsible for his or her own spiritual welfare. The ultimate aim is to pass, through meditation and self-sacrifice, beyond the karmic cycle to reach the spiritual state of *nirvana*, where desire, suffering, and causality finally end. Pious devotees aim to improve their *karma* by following the philosophy of the Four Noble Truths and seeking the moral guidance of the Eightfold Path.

THE FOUR NOBLE TRUTHS

Life is suffering.

Suffering is the result of desire.

It is possible for suffering to cease.

The Noble Eightfold Path will lead to a release from suffering.

THE EIGHTFOLD PATH

Wisdom
- Right view • Right intention

Ethical Conduct
- Right speech • Right action • Right livelihood

Mental Development
- Right effort • Right mindfulness • Right concentration

Buddhism is an important part of daily life in Sri Lanka for around 70 percent of the population; Buddhist temples and the white domes of *dagobas* (stupas) characterize every town and village, while festivals are carried out with great vigor. *Poya* (full moon) days are of particular importance to Buddhists, and are official public holidays.

Since there is no form of organizational or congregational worship, devotees visit their local temples as they wish, lighting candles, making *puja* (prayers and offerings), reciting the *pirith* (Buddhist scriptures), and listening to the ancient truths. Although devotees often bring lotus flowers to offer to the Buddha, he is above all a teacher who offers guidance. Sri Lankan Buddhists also worship a select few Hindu gods who they believe help them to achieve specific aspirations, such as success in a business enterprise or fortune with the harvest.

Hinduism

Approximately 15 percent of the population follow Hinduism. Devotees are mainly Tamils living in the north and east of the island, but there are also followers in Colombo, Kandy, and the tea plantations of the Hill Country. While it is thought that Hinduism was practiced on the island before the arrival of Buddhism, it was not until the later Anuradhapura and early Polonnaruwa periods that it became firmly established by successive Tamil kings.

Hinduism does not follow a book, nor does it have a single founder or religious structure. Despite there being innumerable deities, there is only one god at the heart of the religion—the infinite, formless Brahman. The many deities are actually manifestations of Brahman, and since they represent the many facets of life, such as wealth, fortune, and beauty, they allow people to reach God through many ways. Of the three highest manifestations (*Trimurti*) of Brahman, Siva is particularly venerated by Sri Lankan Tamils. Popular lesser deities include the elephant-headed Ganesh, the goddess of fertility, Pattini, and Kataragama, god of war.

Hinduism is a way of life: the fulfillment of ritual and social duties will enhance a devotee's *karma*. Sri Lankan Hindus often have pictures of their favorite deities in their homes, use idols and images in their daily worship, and regularly visit *devalayas* (shrines dedicated to individual deities) and *kovils* (temples).

Islam
Islam was founded in the seventh century CE by the Prophet Mohammed, and introduced to Sri Lanka a century later by descendants of Arab traders who settled on the island. Comprising 7 percent of the population, Muslims live in separate communities in order to preserve their Islamic culture. Devotees of Islam, a monotheistic faith, pledge to surrender to the will of Allah (God) as revealed to Mohammed and recorded in the Koran.

Sri Lankan Muslims generally follow the Sunni school of Islamic law. The Five Pillars of Islam are: the *shahada*, or creed; prayer five times a day; fasting during Ramadan; almsgiving; and the Hajj, or pilgrimage to Mecca. Each Muslim community is built around a cupola-domed mosque, to which devotees are called five times a day to congregate and pray. The most spiritual day is Friday, when they go to the mosque to observe *Salat-al-Jummah*, or Friday prayers.

Christianity

While some Christians believe that Thomas the Apostle was active in Sri Lanka in the first century CE, it was not until the advent of colonial rule that Christianity had a significant impact on the population. Catholicism, which comprises much of the 7 percent Christian community, remains strong in many western coastal towns and villages, while Our Lady of Madhu Church near Mannar—Sri Lanka's most important Christian site—receives up to 300,000 pilgrims every August.

KARMA

Sri Lankans are more relaxed about missed opportunities than Westerners, because they believe that if something does not work out it was not meant to be, and that it will probably come around again at a more opportune time, with more success. The cause of this attitude is *karma*—the cycle of cause and effect—where an individual's

good or bad deeds determine his or her future.
Both Buddhists and Hindus believe in
reincarnation and that good deeds will improve
one's position in the next life with the goal of
eventually reaching a state of release (*nirvana*).

For Buddhists, all karmic actions result from
mental intent and must be genuine. Even if
someone appears to be professing piety on the
outside but underneath is doing something only
for selfish reasons, it will have a negative effect on a
person's *karma* because it is the fundamental
intention of the action that is key. To Buddhists,
karma is not predetermined or fatalistic: people act
of their own free will to create their own destiny.

THE FAMILY

The family is highly valued in Sri Lankan society,
and is a source of great strength. Among all
ethnicities both the nuclear family and the
extended family are vitally important social units.
The father is typically the head of the household,
while women are responsible for the home and
children, although the civil war has resulted in
many widows having to take the dominant role.
Older family members are valued more highly than
in the West, and typically live with their adult
children in old age.

There is a strong sense of community in most
families; those with good connections will often
help in times of difficulty and assist in finding

even an unqualified member of the family a good job, though by Western standards this practice would be regarded as nepotism. However, for all the strengths that the extended family offers, there are just as many drawbacks and demands.

EDUCATION

Sri Lankans value education greatly as a means of improving one's prospects in life. The Sri Lankan population is highly educated. At nearly 91 percent, the country has one of the highest literacy rates in South Asia. While much of this can be attributed to the free education system that has been in place since 1944, the efforts of postindependence governments to make education from kindergarten to university level one of their highest priorities contributed to a steady rise in literacy rates and educational attainment levels. The medium for instruction in schools is either Sinhalese or Tamil, depending on the locality.

While free education is advantageous, the facilities and equipment in some of the most rural government schools (around 20 percent), especially in the plantation sector, are very poor. Also, some teachers are unwilling to travel the long distances to reach the most isolated communities. Many parents pay for private tutors to supplement their children's education and prepare them for important exams, feeling that their children's advancement in learning will also give them increased security for the future. Wealthier families send their children to private or international schools, where the facilities are often first-class.

THE URBAN–RURAL DIVIDE

Sri Lanka is traditionally an agrarian society. Three-quarters of the population live in rural towns and villages (*gamma*) scattered throughout the island. Many Sri Lankans who have migrated to the cities for educational or employment opportunities still have a very close bond with their rural home areas, and escape back there as often as they can. The richer urban population have grown increasingly Westernized in their standard and style of living, while the rural villages, especially the most isolated ones, remain the island's cultural heartland, where traditional familial values and attitudes still predominate.

Sri Lankans living in rural areas are generally more conservative, certainly in dress and behavior, than most city dwellers. Although this is not always the case, many village girls have more traditional aspirations than their richer urban counterparts, looking forward to finding a suitable husband and starting a family rather than embarking on an exciting working career. While many upper-class city dwellers regard their country neighbors' ingrained traditions and slower pace of life as backward and inferior, the rural villagers often regard them in return as immoral and condescending.

ATTITUDES TOWARD WOMEN

Sri Lankan society is still influenced by traditional patriarchal values, whereby women are respected more as mothers and homemakers than for the prestige of their job status. Clear distinctions, especially in rural areas, are still made in the roles of the sexes so that household work, raising children, and cooking are seen as women's work, while men are the providers and protectors of the family. Over the last few decades, however, and as a consequence of the civil war and the devastating tsunami of December 2004, women now head more than one-fifth of Sri Lankan households. A feminist drive has resulted in the creation of a number of organizations offering support for women both in the workplace and at home.

Sri Lankan women are more fortunate than their Asian sisters, since their access to education and the subsequent high literacy rate has resulted in their having access to numerous economic opportunities unmatched in other Asian countries. State-funded schooling removed many of the barriers, particularly for poorer families, that had previously limited education for girls. A good education is also increasingly seen as an added qualification for marriage.

While men and women hold equal rights under national, civil, and criminal constitutional laws, men are sometimes preferred over women as employees, and tend to have a disproportionate representation in the most powerful decision-making positions. In civil disputes such as land inheritance, marriage, and divorce, many of the archaic personal laws still favor men. Even though the country was the first in the world to have a female prime minister and has also had a female president, women's political representation is one of the worst in Asia, despite their forming half of the electorate. Universal suffrage was granted in 1931.

Young girls in the household tend to assume their female roles from an early age, learning to adopt a demure demeanor in social situations. Sex before marriage is taboo—although in reality it might happen in secret—and relations between men and women are formal except between members of the extended family and long-term friends. Since women have more social responsibilities than men, girls are more strictly guarded than boys. In the cities—especially in Colombo—among the more Westernized upper classes, girls and boys mix freely.

ATTITUDES TOWARD OTHERS
Sri Lankans have learned to live with plurality. Despite the civil war, relations between ethnic groups are generally good away from the conflict

zones. Physical differences between ethnicities are almost invisible—Tamils are believed to be darker-skinned than the Sinhalese, but this is not always the case—and often the only barrier to relationships is language. All Sri Lankans have a similar core of cultural beliefs and values, especially in the fields of religion and family. Intermarriage is becoming more common, and friends and families often share celebrations, cuisine, and religious festivals across ethnic divisions.

Since history has favored one or more ethnic group at one time or another, hostility and competition for political and economic power have periodically occurred. However, it should be remembered that the origins of the country's civil conflict are politically rather than socially motivated, being the result of a string of Sinhalese Buddhist-oriented policies of postindependence governments that marginalized the Tamil community. The LTTE is a Tamil militant organization, and should not be identified with the majority of Tamil people. While it is true that relations between the Sinhalese and the Tamils have been strained by the civil war, away from the conflict zones most live in harmony with one another as neighbors, colleagues, and friends.

The Muslims are on good terms with all ethnic groups, although they tend to keep more to themselves to preserve and protect their religion and culture, inhabiting separate villages or certain urban districts. Since they form more of a social presence in the north and east, where their numbers are higher, they have also been caught up in the civil war.

Attitudes Toward Foreigners

Sri Lankans enjoy meeting and conversing with foreigners, many of whom come to Sri Lanka on vacation. They are a warmhearted, talkative, and inquisitive people, and often invite visitors home to meet their families and friends. While the warmth and welcome are nearly always genuine, there are a few Sri Lankans who see foreigners as a possible gateway to material gain, and may want to make an acquaintance if they think there might be some advantage in it for themselves.

There are plenty of foreigners in Colombo and the main tourist resorts, but this is not the case in rural villages. Having seen little change over the decades, country people may not understand why their values and beliefs are not shared by their foreign visitors. However, they are eager to befriend those who show genuine respect for the Sri Lankan culture.

PRIDE AND "SAVING FACE"

Sri Lankans are a proud people. They are proud of their history, their country, their achievements, and their democratic traditions in the face of the myriad political and social challenges over the years. They are also especially proud of their cricket players, who are revered as royalty throughout the country.

Sri Lankan Independence Day (February 4) has great significance, and is celebrated with pageants and parades of much pomp and ceremony.

As in most of Asia, emotional displays of any type are uncommon in public, where it is important to save "face" in social situations; on a Western level, this roughly translates as maintaining one's dignity in public. Face is much easier to lose than to keep, and it is of huge consequence to individuals when it is lost. Saving face is something Sri Lankans do to preserve not only their own dignity but also that of others; for example, by accepting assistance from someone even if help is not needed, or by taking care to lodge a complaint against a colleague in private rather than in front of his peers.

Sri Lankans will go to great lengths to avoid losing face, as this is seen as preferable to admitting they are unable or unwilling to do something. While this can be frustrating, since decisions are often avoided altogether for fear of failure, it is also endearing, as it is done out of a natural desire to oblige. When Sri Lankans are asked a question to which the answer should be "no," many will give noncommittal, vague, or even positive answers to avoid disappointing the questioner or admitting that they cannot do something.

ATTITUDES TOWARD WORK

Most Sri Lankans are hard workers who are honest in the workplace, dedicated to their job, and motivated by opportunities to improve their position. However, there are some who prefer a job more for the prestige of its title than for the actual work that it involves. Sri Lankans are entrepreneurs, and many dream of owning their own business.

What appears to Westerners to be nepotism sometimes occurs in the Sri Lankan workplace, mainly in family businesses where younger family members may be promoted above others despite lack of experience, education, or management skills. Relatives are seen as more loyal, and therefore more trustworthy. In larger businesses this practice is not so common, and while "help" might be given to members of their extended family by those in a position to do so, it would not be at the expense of others who have achieved their job positions on merit.

ATTITUDES TOWARD TIME

Since the pace of life in Sri Lanka is much slower than in the West, Sri Lankans are more relaxed when it comes to time. Schedules are often subject to delay, especially where public holidays and festivals intervene, congested roads disrupt journeys, and many things take longer to accomplish. However, Sri Lankans have learned to account for this by being realistic in most areas of their timekeeping and by leaving manageable gaps between appointments. A Sri Lankan may be ten to twenty minutes late for a meeting—rarely more—but you are expected to arrive on time, as this signifies respect. If you are meeting a Sri Lankan friend or colleague and realise that you are going to be late, it would be polite to call to let them know.

PUBLIC DISPLAYS OF AFFECTION
As we have seen, Sri Lankans behave very conservatively in public. It is uncommon for couples, even when married, to kiss and hug in public. One often sees members of the same sex holding hands—especially young men—but this signifies friendship rather than sexual preference.

HOMOSEXUALITY
Homosexuality is illegal in Sri Lanka. Most homosexual couples keep this aspect of their lives secret, especially from their families, and open up only to close friends. While Sri Lankans are bound by negative cultural and religious proscriptions of homosexuality, it is present in every level of society. An increasingly vocal gay community is lobbying for reform.

chapter three

CUSTOMS & TRADITIONS

Festivals are an important part of daily life in Sri Lanka for every religion, bringing people together and strengthening relationships between family and friends. Many occasions, including rites of passage, are governed by auspicious times, hallowed by tradition, and celebrated with festive food. Every major festival of each faith is represented in the public holiday calendar, which combined with every Buddhist full moon day (*poya*) means that there are no fewer than twenty-five public holidays a year. While banks and offices are closed on public holidays and everyone is entitled to a day off work, some shops and enterprises may remain open, especially if the festival is not enjoined by the owner's faith; for example, a Muslim shop may continue to do business on a *poya* day.

POYA DAYS

Since ancient times Asian spiritual leaders have made a point of engaging in religious observances and refraining from worldly pursuits on full moon days. The Buddha later adopted this practice and when Buddhism was introduced to Sri Lanka in the third century BCE, poya days also became part of the island's tradition. The Sinhalese word *poya* is derived from the Sanskrit word *upavasam*, which, loosely, means a day of fasting and religious observance.

While each *poya* day, known by its traditional Sinhalese name, is related to an incident in the life of the Buddha, it is also significant of a (nonchronologically ordered) historic Buddhist event in Sri Lanka. The most important lunar month is Vesak (May), which is celebrated by Buddhists all over the world; Poson (June) comes a close second.

On *poya* days practicing Buddhists dress in white to visit the temple (*pansala*) for the rituals of worship where they pray, meditate, and listen to religious discourses. Ceremonies are conducted from dawn to dusk at all temples. The most devoted Buddhists observe the eight precepts and, after noon, abstain from food and all forms of entertainment and luxury. Buddhist sermons and discussions are broadcast on national TV and radio.

Poya days are public holidays when many businesses are closed and the sale of alcohol and meat is strictly forbidden. Beside their significance to Buddhists, full moon days are also important to Hindus. Those of other faiths enjoy this observance by taking a relaxing day off work.

SRI LANKAN FESTIVALS
While Sri Lanka is predominantly a Buddhist country, sizeable Hindu, Muslim, and Christian

populations have resulted in Sri Lanka having one of the highest number of festivals a year in the world. Since most festivals follow the lunar calendar, where a full moon signifies the start of the lunar month, rather than the Gregorian calendar recognized by the West, some festival dates vary considerably from year to year.

Buddhist Festivals

Buddhist festivals typically revolve around *poya* days, of which there are typically twelve a year; one extra lunar month is added every two or three

years to keep the solar and lunar calendars in check. Buddhist festivals are visual and colorful events that often involve weeks of preparation. The biggest festivals are celebrated with *peraheras*—

processions of dancers, drummers, singers, costumed elephants, and fire walkers—the largest and most famous of which is the ten-day Kandy Esala Perahera in July or August.

Hindu Festivals

Hindu festivals are numerous. Many are local, rather than national, and many take place in the temples of the Jaffna Peninsula. Characterized by color and light, Hindu festivals are sometimes marked by the self-mortification of pious devotees as an act of faith or atonement.

Muslim Festivals

Muslim festivals are observed by special prayers in the mosque followed by celebrations at home. They also follow the lunar calendar, but since extra months are not added the dates of these festivals move back at a rate of about eleven days a year. The most important Muslim festivals—Milad un-Nabi (the Prophet's birthday), Id ul-Fitr (the end of Ramadan), and Id ul-Allah (the beginning of the pilgrimage season to Mecca)—are all public holidays.

Christian Festivals

Although only a small proportion of the country is Christian, Western influence, especially in the cities and the tourist areas, has resulted in Christmas, for example, being noticeably celebrated in Sri Lanka. Christmas trees and cards, inflatable Santas, festive hats, and lights are sold at roadside stalls and in the bigger, highly decorated city malls weeks before the event itself. Passion plays are enacted in the Catholic communities during Easter.

THE FESTIVE YEAR
January
Duruthu Poya commemorates the Buddha's first visit to Sri Lanka. The event is marked by a

spectacular triple *perahera* at the Raja Maha Vihara temple in Kelaniya.

Thai Pongol is a Hindu festival that coincides

with the end of the rice harvest. It is a two-day festival to thank the sun god Surya for his part in bestowing a successful yield. The first day is a public holiday.

February
Navam Poya commemorates the Buddha's announcement of his impending death and nirvana. It is celebrated with a major *perahera* at the Gangaramaya Temple in Colombo.

Maha Sivarathri is held in February or March and is an important Hindu festival dedicated to Lord Siva. Pilgrims keep overnight vigils in temples by singing hymns, saying prayers, and fasting. It is a national holiday.

March
Medin Poya commemorates the Buddha's first visit to his parental home following his attaining enlightenment.

April
Bak Poya commemorates the Buddha's second visit to Sri Lanka.

Sri Lankan New Year is typically held on April 13 and 14, although its exact timing changes every year. Known as Aluth Avurudhu in Sinhala, or Puththandu in Tamil, this is a festival celebrated by Sinhalese and Tamils in their own unique way. It is a nonreligious celebration that marks the Sri Lankan New Year according to the solar calendar. The New Year signifies renewal, and houses are vigorously cleaned in preparation for the event; special food, especially sweet delicacies, are prepared; and presents, usually new clothes, are exchanged. Auspicious times signify the traditional carrying out of rituals while tribute is paid to elders. Businesses close for up to a week as many celebrants visit friends and family. It is a two-day public holiday.

Good Friday commemorates the death and resurrection of Jesus Christ. It is one of the most important Christian events, and many Catholic churches mark the occasion with passion plays and *peraheras*. It is an official public holiday.

May
Vesak Poya is for Buddhists the most important lunar month of the year, since it commemorates the triple anniversary of the Buddha's birth, enlightenment, and passing. It is especially significant for Sri Lankan Buddhists since it is when the Buddha paid his third and final visit to the island. This two-day festival and public holiday is marked by colorful illuminated lanterns displayed outside nearly every Buddhist home and business. Huge *pandols*—electronically lit platforms that display scenes from

the life of the Buddha—are erected in towns, while food stalls (*dansalas*) distribute free food and soft drinks. White-clothed devotees flock to the temples to meditate, pray, and fast.

Republic Day or **National Heroes Day** on May 22 commemorates Ceylon's becoming the Republic of Sri Lanka in 1972, and honors all the Sri Lankan soldiers who have died in the civil war.

June
Since it commemorates the introduction of Buddhism to Sri Lanka, **Poson Poya** is the second-most important Buddhist festival after Vesak. Devotees flock to Anuradhapura and Mihintale, the site where King Devanampiyatissa and his advisors were converted to Buddhism in 247 BCE.

July
Esala Poya commemorates the Buddha's first sermon since gaining enlightenment and also the arrival of the Buddha's Tooth Relic in Sri Lanka in the fourth century CE. While there are numerous nationwide celebrations in the month of Esala,

 including one at Kataragama, Kandy's world-famous ten-day pageant is the most spectacular and reflects the city's prestige in safeguarding the

customs and traditions

ancient tooth relic. Every night as many as a hundred bejeweled and illuminated elephants flanked by throngs of dancers, drummers, acrobats, and stilt walkers attract crowds in their thousands.

Usually held in either July or August, **Vel**, the most visual of Sri Lanka's Hindu festivals, is held in Colombo and commemorates the victory of Lord Murukan over the forces of evil. An ornate silver chariot bearing a statue of Murukan (or the war god Skanda) is born from Pettah to Bambalapitiya and accompanied by scores of colorfully dressed pilgrims, dancers, musicians, and caparisoned elephants.

August
Nikini Poya marks the beginning of a three-month retreat (*vas*) for the monastic community.

Jaffna's **Nallur Festival** is a Hindu celebration in honor of the war god Skanda. Lasting twenty-five days, this is the island's longest festival. Huge chariot processions are enhanced by drumming and dancing while particularly enthusiastic devotees perform acts of self-mortification, such as driving silver spears or hooks through their bodies, in the belief that the gods will protect them from pain.

September
Binara Poya commemorates the Buddha's visit to heaven to preach to his mother and the celestial multitude.

While the Hindu festival of **Dussehra** honors the supreme warrior goddess Durga, it also commemorates Rama's victory over the demon king Ravana in the legendary Indian epic *Ramayana*. Oil lamps are lit to invoke the blessings of Lakshmi, the Hindu goddess of wealth.

October
Vap Poya commemorates the conclusion of the Buddha's preaching in the heavenly realm and his return to earth as well as the end of the monastic period of fasting.

Deepavali, or the **Festival of Lights** (Diwali) is a Hindu festival that symbolizes the victory of good over evil. It is marked by the lighting of lamps and lanterns in Tamil homes and places of worship. It is a public holiday.

November
Il Poya commemorates the Buddha's ordination of sixty disciples to disperse his teachings.

December
Unduwap Poya commemorates the planting in Anuradhapura in 288 BCE of the sacred bo sapling brought from India by Emperor Asoka's daughter, Sangamitta, who also established the Bhikkhuni (Order of the Nuns). This sapling is said to have

been taken from the historical bodhi tree under which the Buddha gained enlightenment in Bodhi Gaya, India. It is now one of the oldest documented living trees in the world.

NATIONAL HOLIDAYS	
February 4	Independence Day
May 1	Labor Day
December 25	Christmas Day

CELEBRATING WITH FOOD

While Sri Lankan cuisine is renowned for being hot and spicy, the part it plays in celebrations is better known for its symbolism than for its flavor. For Buddhists and Hindus the sharing of food between family and close friends symbolizes the importance of reconciliation and harmony, while for Muslims, who often eat from the same plate, or *sahan* (which serves six persons), its importance lies in the equality of the community. Rice, a symbol of life and fertility, is the main food used in nearly every ceremonial occasion alongside more contemporary sweet foods.

For Buddhists, most celebrations begin with the preparation of *kiribath* (rice cooked in coconut milk); it is a baby's first solid meal, it is the first food that the bride and groom share, and it is ritually prepared at the opening of a new business venture or when a couple moves into their new home, to ensure a lucky and propitious beginning. It is also the first meal eaten after the

Sri Lankan New Year has dawned, often accompanied by *kaung* (sweet oil cake), *kokis* (deep-fried biscuits), and bananas.

For Hindus, *kiribath*, often boiled with *jaggery*—a coarse brown sugar made from the *kithul* palm—is also prepared for special occasions. At Thai Pongol all family members add a few morsels of rice to the boiling coconut milk to offer to the sun god in thanksgiving for the rice harvest. Pongol means "boiling over," and as the milk overflows it signifies abundance or prosperity. Buddhists perform a similar ritual at New Year and on other occasions that mark a new beginning.

Another ritualistic act performed by Buddhists is for the host to place a full glass of water on a tray and offer it to guests, who respond by lightly touching it. This act indicates that the meal will be served and that everyone is invited to share in the occasion. Guests touch the glass to signify their appreciation at being invited to join in with the celebrations.

ASTROLOGY AND AUSPICIOUS TIMING
Astrology plays a significant role in the lives of nearly all Sri Lankans, most significantly Buddhist

and Hindus, although it is a belief based on tradition rather than religion. Astrologers are highly regarded, and are nearly always consulted before Sri Lankans embark on any significant enterprise in their personal, professional, or private lives, since they can foretell good or bad days according to a person's individual horoscope that is cast shortly after birth.

When Buddhist and Hindu children are born, the exact time, to the nearest minute, is recorded, as well as the date, so that an astrologer may use this information to cast a personal horoscope. The horoscope is then used by astrologers to help an individual move toward a prosperous life by suggesting good, appropriate, or auspicious times to commence tasks. If someone is venturing into a new business, for example, an astrologer will be consulted and he will suggest an auspicious day and time for it to start, according to the horoscope of that individual. Rural people in particular have great faith in astrology, and it plays a dominant role in agriculture, especially in the cultivation of rice.

Auspicious times are used in rites of passage, such as in determining the best day and time for a baby to be fed its first solid meal, and for when a child should go to school for the first time. For many aspects of marriage, such as the most auspicious times for the wedding date and the registration, both parties' horoscopes are considered. Astrology also plays a significant role in cultural events, none more so than Sri Lankan

New Year, when nearly every ritual is carried out at an auspicious time.

AYURVEDA AND HERBAL MEDICINE

The Ayurveda is an ancient Hindu system of medicine (from the Sanskrit *ayur*, life, and *veda*, knowledge) practiced in India and Sri Lanka that regards an illness as the result of an imbalance in a person's basic makeup. It seeks to cure disease by rectifying imbalances over time, through the examination of the whole of a patient's lifestyle, habits, diet, and emotional proclivities in order to find the root of the disease. Remedies come in a range of lotions, tablets, ointments, and oils, while therapeutic massages, healing wraps, and special diets are also commonly prescribed.

More than 75 percent of the Sri Lankan population believe that the ancient system of Ayurveda and the administration of herbal remedies are complementary to Western medicinal practices, and indeed they coexist happily side by side. For many, herbal medicines and Ayurvedic practitioners are also a cheaper alternative to visiting a Western doctor, and no less effective, since even conditions such as hypertension, rheumatism, and arthritis have been known to respond well to herbal treatments.

SUPERSTITIONS AND OMENS

Sri Lanka is a superstitious society. There is widespread belief in good or bad omens, such as whom you may meet at a particular time of the day, what they might say to you, or even what they might be carrying. Certain days of the week are considered ominous, animals are seen as omens of good or bad fortune, while death has numerous superstitions surrounding it.

SUPERSTITIONS SURROUNDING DEATH

- When brought to the funeral home, the body is always placed facing west. No one chooses to sleep in this direction normally.
- At least one person is present with the body at all times of the day or night, to prevent evil spirits from taking up residence in the house.
- Pictures are turned upside down so that the people in the photographs will not be possessed by the spirits of the dead.
- The body is always taken out of the funeral house feet first in order to disorient the spirit and prevent it from returning.
- The dead are never buried or cremated on a Friday, as this is thought to have a devastating effect on the surviving family members.

Amulets, charms, and thread bracelets are worn by superstitious persons to ward off the Evil Eye. Newborn babies in Buddhist families wear the

Pancha-uda (a gold or silver pendant embellished with five weapons—the bow and arrow, the conch, the sword, the trident, and the disc) until they are old enough to go to school. Hindus traditionally place a spot or *potthu*, marked in red or black paste, on a baby's forehead to protect it from the Evil Eye.

When a person becomes ill, malicious spirits, or *yakkas*, are sometimes blamed, because they are believed to be capable of bringing about pathological states of the body and mind. Healing ceremonies (*tovils*) are carried out by exorcists (*kattadiyas*) to drive away these spirits through charms, offerings, and threats. Rituals can go on throughout the night.

RITES OF PASSAGE
Each community has its own ceremonies for important occasions, such as birth, marriage, and death, which may be either social or religious in nature. According to each family's individual beliefs, desires, and financial means, these are celebrated either publicly or privately.

Birth and Early Childhood
Sri Lankans cherish children, so the birth of a baby, whether boy or girl, is a very important event. In the case of Buddhist and Hindu children, the exact time and date of the birth is recorded, and an astrologer is summoned to cast a horoscope, indicate an auspicious time for the child's naming ceremony, and give the first letter, or choice of letters, of the child's name.

According to Hindu tradition, soon after a birth the family goes through a period of ceremonial impurity for thirty-one days (although it can be shorter if there is an event already scheduled in the family), during which time they refrain from taking part in any religious ceremonies, including visiting the temple. After this a religious ceremony is performed and sandalwood paste is applied to the baby's newly shaved head after a bath. Also unique to Sri Lankan Hindus is the preparation of sweet *kolukattai*—crescent-shaped dough decorated with pieces of coconut to resemble teeth—to mark the occasion of the child's teething.

The Muslims have their own traditions. Since they do not believe in astrology, horoscopes are not cast. Instead, the first utterances a baby should hear are the *Azan*—the call to prayer—and the *Iqma*—the answer to prayer. After seven days the baby's head is shaved and a name is chosen, which is customarily of Arabic origin and after the name of a prophet.

A child's first solid food is typically *kiribath*, and the occasion is symbolically celebrated. Sinhalese families perform this custom seven months after birth, and consult an astrologer for an auspicious date and time for the occasion.

There is also an event to mark a child's advent into the world of learning. At the age of three or four, a ceremony is held whereby a teacher, priest, or learned elder in the family teaches the child to say and write the first letters of the Sinhalese or Tamil alphabet.

Coming of Age

A girl's coming of age is celebrated after her first menstrual period, more commonly known as the occasion of her becoming a "big girl." While in past times this would have signified her availability on the marriage market, today it is an excuse for a party, where the traditional rituals are followed by gift giving and fun.

When a girl has her first period, she is customarily kept inside the house for about a week, seeing only her close family, not attending school, and eating only vegetarian food. The date of the coming ceremony is set by an astrologer. The rituals start in the early morning, when the girl is bathed in holy water laced with jasmine flowers by an elder of the family, followed by the lighting of oil lamps and the meal of *kiribath* to mark her entrance into the adult world. Then the day is spent with the extended family and the party is held in the evening.

There is no specific rite of passage for boys.

Marriage Customs

Marriages in Sri Lanka are a sacred bond and a natural progression in a person's life. Arranged marriages still take place, especially among Hindu families; however, "love matches," where young people choose their own partners, are becoming increasingly common. Caste is still a significant factor, while the matching of a couple's horoscopes—planetary compatibility—is of vital import. The legal age for marriage is eighteen.

Once a marriage has been agreed on, Buddhists and Hindus consult an astrologer, who sets a date for the wedding. The basic rituals and customs of each religion are thereafter adhered to while the extent of the celebrations varies according to the social and financial status of the families involved. If possible, couples will have two celebrations—a wedding and a homecoming—the latter being symbolic of the bride's arrival at her marital home. Alcohol will not be served at a Muslim wedding since it is forbidden under Islamic law.

A Buddhist wedding is a social union. Kandyan ceremonies are the most elaborate in dress and ritual. The main ceremony, which is centered on the beautifully decorated bridal platform (*poruwa*), is not religious, and is carried out by a master of ceremonies. The registration of the marriage may take place either before or after the *poruwa* ceremony, and is the only part that is legally binding.

At the auspicious time, the bride and groom step on to the *poruwa* and the ceremony commences. Gifts, food, and betel leaves are given and exchanged between the couple and their families, while verses in Sinhala, Sanskrit, and Pali are read out to invoke the blessings of the deities. The most significant part of the ceremony is when the index fingers of the bride and groom are tied together with golden thread to symbolize the bond of marriage.

Hindu weddings are conducted by a priest and reflect the sacred union of the couple. They involve many symbolic rituals, including the giving by the groom to the bride of a *thaali* (gold necklace) and *koorai* (sari) during the ceremony itself. The ceremony takes place around a fire symbolizing Brahman, which

the bride and groom must circle seven times to demonstrate their commitment and union.

A Muslim ceremony is both a social and a religious event, which typically consists of two parts: the *nikah*, or signing of the marriage contract in the mosque, and the *waleema*, the ceremony that marks the consummation of the marriage. After the customary rituals have concluded, guests are often treated to a lavish feast, and celebrations may go on for days.

It is common for mixed-faith unions to marry with the customs of both religions.

Death

Each religious group observes its own customary funeral rites; Buddhists and Hindus prefer to cremate their dead, while Christians always bury theirs in order to facilitate their resurrection. Muslims also prefer to bury their dead, doing so without a coffin and in shallow graves, and this is done within twenty-four hours of the death.

In most cases except that of Muslims, the deceased lies in an open coffin in a "funeral house" (the home or family of the deceased) for a set number of days, to allow friends and family to pay their respects. Oil candles are lit and windows are kept open for both superstitious and sanitary reasons.

When it is time for the funeral ceremony Hindu families surround the coffin, place oil on the deceased's head, and put rice and flowers inside the coffin. People wear light-colored clothing and often follow the coffin to the cemetery or burial ground on foot.

Most funerals are attended by the whole family and by everyone who knew the deceased; however Muslim and Hindu women (if it is a cremation) are not permitted to be present. A person who did not directly know the deceased—such as a friend of the deceased's close relations—may also attend the funeral to give support to the bereaved. Posters of the deceased are customarily pasted on to walls, while white flags strung along fences and roadsides provide a guided path to the funeral ceremony.

After the funeral is over, families continue their vigil in the house, with the windows open, until seven days have elapsed. On the final day Buddhists offer *dana*, or alms, to monks. This practice —an offering whose merits it is hoped will be transferred to the dead—is performed again after three months, and yet again after a year, to mark the first anniversary of the death.

chapter four

MAKING FRIENDS

Friendships in Sri Lanka tend to be forged at an early age. While the extended family is where most socializing takes place, people typically have a close circle of trusted friends from their school and village with whom they remain close throughout life, even if they don't see each other often. Loyalty and commitment are vital social obligations between friends, while patience, friendliness, courtesy, and restraint are highly valued virtues that instill both respect and confidence.

Very close friends are generally regarded in the same light as family, and within the circle they will do their utmost to help each other out when in need. While trust can take a long time to earn, especially if you are quite unknown (not only foreigners but also those from outside the family or social network), it can take seconds to lose, particularly if it involves pride or a loss of face. Wrongdoing between long-term friends is more easily forgiven.

Society is largely segregated by gender. Women, especially in more conservative rural areas, are confined to spending much of their time at home, while men are more likely to be out of the house, socializing in groups. Social norms dictate that women and men, unless they are blood relations or close family friends, do not socialize freely; it is taboo for a boy and a girl to spend private time together if their families are not related by blood or close friendship. It is therefore common for friendships outside the family circle to be between members of the same sex.

The Westernized upper classes, however, socialize in a similar way to the West, and dating is not uncommon. Boys and girls mix freely in bars and clubs, go to parties and restaurants, and either as a couple or in a group take weekend trips to the beach or the hills.

GREETINGS

While forms of greeting and methods of communication may vary between different ethnic groups, each possessing its own cultural nuances, the most important rules of social etiquette are universal. Forms of address, spatial distance, and intimacy typically mark differences in social rank. Eye contact is important, demonstrating interest and trust.

On formal occasions the Sinhalese traditionally greet each other by saying "*Ayubowan*," which means "May you be blessed with a long life." This word is accompanied by clasping the palms together, as if in prayer, close to the chest, and a slight bow or nod of the head, similar to the Indian *namaste*. It is considered polite to return the gesture. Tamils customarily greet people by saying "*Vanakkam*," which has a similar meaning, while Muslims say "*Assalamu Alaikum*," the traditional Islamic greeting that means "Peace be upon you."

On informal occasions, just "Hello" is commonly said. In relaxed social settings, and especially among younger friends and acquaintances, Sri Lankans often say "*Kohomeda*?" which means, "How are you?" accompanied by a handshake, sometimes a head waggle, and often a broad smile. Close friends of the same sex, both male and female, may also give each other a quick hug or pat on the back and remain holding hands even after the initial handshake is over.

While handshakes, especially in business, are widely considered normal in modern-day Sri Lanka, visitors should be aware that since women tend to refrain from physical contact with men from outside their families, it is polite for a man to shake a woman's hand only when she offers it. Since kissing is believed to be an intimate, and therefore private, form of affection, the "social" kiss, as a form of greeting, is uncommon. Family members may greet each other by touching cheek-to-cheek.

Sri Lankans address people respectfully, by using their appropriate title followed by their surname. This is an acknowledgement of the status or seniority of that person. For this reason, it is better to wait for the other party to move to first-name terms before you do. Sri Lankans often greet each other using nicknames or relationship terms such as *Mali*, which means younger brother, or *Nangi*, younger sister, or other titles such as *Mahattaya*, Sir, or *Nona*, Madam, in preference to using first names.

A Natural Curiosity

Sri Lankans love asking questions. They are keen to learn about the country and culture of their foreign guests, as well as to hear their opinions of Sri Lanka. It is not uncommon for a foreigner to walk down the street and be asked "What is your country?" and "What is your name?" by curious Sri Lankans, who may be looking not only for the information but also for the cultural exchange and the chance to practice some English.

When greeting Buddhist monks, laypeople use a different form of address—"*Hamuduruwo*"—which is respectful and polite. They may also kneel down on the ground with head bowed as a mark of submission and respect. Children also perform this gesture as a mark of respect to their parents or elders. It is customary to bring ritual offerings of sacred betel leaves, areca nuts, and lime paste when visiting the Veddah community.

MEETING SRI LANKANS

When engaging a Sri Lankan in conversation it is important not to be overenthusiastic. Be friendly, but also a little reserved, so that your sincerity is never in doubt. Making a good impression is vital, especially in business, when it might lead to an ongoing relationship. While eye contact is important in showing trust, remember that some Sri Lankans (such as Muslim women) might avoid this form of communication, either out of modesty or simply because they are shy—shy to speak English or because they might not be accustomed to meeting people from foreign cultures. The famous Sri Lankan smile often signifies welcome and warmth, but sometimes it covers embarrassment or confusion.

Sri Lanka is divided ethnically, politically, and by social status, so if you don't know someone well it is best to avoid controversial topics such as politics and sexuality. The best and safest topics to talk about are your family, your country, and what you do for a living. Sri Lankans are proud of their homeland, and your positive impressions of it will be very much appreciated. Similarly asking questions about their family will also make a good impression since, as we have seen, the family unit is of the utmost importance in Sri Lankan society. Appearing genuinely interested is the key to success.

Sri Lankans have a sense of humor, and are eager to use it. They are practical jokers, and enjoying teasing each other; but this is rarely intended to hurt the other person. Even when meeting someone for the first time there is no reason why you shouldn't use humor, but it will only be appreciated if it is universally accepted to be funny.

Directness is not common among Sri Lankans, who appear to have an aversion to the word "No," since it might cause disappointment. They also have a tendency to skirt around a point. Sometimes this means that disagreements between Sri Lankans that have been simmering below the surface will suddenly flare up, but anger, when aroused, is usually quickly diffused. Assertiveness is considered rude and aggressive.

With a little understanding, cultural gaps can be bridged. While you may never think exactly as a Sri Lankan does, you may come to a point when you can agree to disagree, with both parties making allowances for the other's different views. It is important to be polite and sensitive to cultural differences, since a reciprocation of common courtesies will allow you true engagement in Sri Lankan society. Since Sri Lankans are genuinely friendly, your chance meeting in a restaurant, on the beach, in a temple, or even on a train could turn into an invitation home, and from that into a lifelong friendship.

INVITATIONS HOME

Sri Lankans are very hospitable. If you have made some new Sri Lankan friends who want to get to know you better, or would like you to meet their families, they may well extend an invitation to their homes. You should accept it!

Bring them a present, but there is no hard and fast rule about what this should be. A dessert item such as ice cream is appreciated, as are chocolates, cookies, or fruit. Wrapped gifts are always put aside to be opened later. A gift of flowers is not appreciated as it is in the Western world, and alcohol, such as a bottle of wine, should be given only if you know the family well. Women generally do not drink. Of course, you should not give alcohol if your hosts are Muslim.

In most households shoes should be removed before entering. If refreshments are offered it is impolite to refuse. If the invitation is for lunch or dinner, the menu is most likely to include rice, accompanied by an assortment of curries, sambols, and salads, as well as a dessert of fruit salad or ice cream. In Muslim homes a dinner of *buriyani* and roast chicken is a popular choice for guests.

Sri Lankans are experts at hospitality and take pleasure from their guests' enjoyment. The meal is expertly prepared in advance by the women of the household, and informally laid out on a table, buffet-style. In traditional homes the men often eat with the guests while the women, who pop in and out of the kitchen to refill curry bowls, eat later. Food may be spooned liberally onto your plate, so if you have had enough, a polite refusal accompanied by a compliment about the cooking will satisfy your hosts that you have enjoyed the meal. Water is typically offered after the meal, as well as perhaps soft drinks and tea, depending on the occasion and the time of day.

Sri Lankans eat rice and curry using their fingers, believing that this heightens the taste of the dish. If you want to do the same, your hosts will definitely approve. Use only the fingertips of your right hand to mix the curry and rice lightly into small bite-sized heaps to pop into your mouth. Avoid getting your palm and the rest of your fingers messy, as this is considered impolite. Wash your hands before and after eating. Most Sri Lankans, however, even those in rural villages, will recognize that foreigners do not all share this custom of eating with their fingers, and will put out cutlery for their guests to use.

If you know a Sri Lankan Buddhist well, you may be invited for an almsgiving in their home— occasions when monks are invited to give a sermon for a deceased family member three months or a year after their passing. Alms in the form of food are given first to the monk and then to friends and family in order to bestow merit on the departed soul. Traditionally a rice and curry buffet is laid out on mats on the floor for everyone to help themselves. It is customary to bring a simple gift of sugar, milk powder, or cookies.

When their guests are leaving, Sri Lankans will wave good-bye from their doorstep until they are completely out of view.

DRESS

Both traditional and Western styles of dress are common in Sri Lanka. Sri Lankans take pride in their appearance and appreciate others who do so. Women, especially in rural areas, cover up much more than those in the Western world, typically wearing long dresses and shirts with sleeves when they are out of their homes.

While the men jump around on the beach often wearing nothing more than their underwear, women swim fully clothed. Western women are not expected to do the same, and bikinis are a common sight in tourist resorts, as are skimpy tops, short skirts, and shorts.

Such clothing may be acceptable wear for the beach, but when in towns and visiting temples and people's homes more modest dress should be worn. The more revealing a woman's clothing, the more unwanted attention she will receive from Sri Lankan men, who may mistake her taste in clothes for promiscuity.

Weddings and other important social functions are occasions to look one's best. Saris are still the preferred formal dress of women, but today have many modern variations. Westernized outfits such as dresses and high heels are gaining in popularity with the younger generation. Men wear suits or smart trousers, shirts, and ties for formal occasions.

chapter five

SRI LANKANS AT HOME

Sri Lanka is traditionally an agrarian society, and approximately three-quarters of the population still live in the rural areas. Those who have migrated to the cities in search of employment retain close ties with their villages through their family and land ownership.

Housing varies greatly according to socioeconomic status and location. In poorer rural areas people may live in settlements that have remained largely unchanged since ancient times, in wattle and daub structures with mud

floors and thatched roofs, while urban Sri Lankans might live in high-rise apartments. A great many buildings remain from the colonial era, some of which have been beautifully restored.

A typical Sri Lankan house is characterized by whitewashed (or sometimes candy-colored) brick walls, red polished cement floors, and windows with built-in vents to allow for the circulation of air. Roofs are tiled or made of corrugated iron. Houses have one to four rooms, a central living area, and a kitchen and laundry room typically located at the back. Front and back verandas are encircled by a garden filled with colorful potted plants and fruit trees.

The interior is usually very simple. Plastic chairs and tables are common and are a cheaper alternative to wood. The pictures on the walls are usually family photos, a calendar, and a religious image elevated above a small shrine, where residents light candles and incense and say prayers. A vase of plastic flowers may provide color. Televisions are becoming increasingly common.

THE HOUSEHOLD AND EXTENDED FAMILY

Among all ethnic groups in Sri Lanka, both the nuclear family and the extended family are vital social units. The extended family is an important social network that provides support to the nuclear family—even newlyweds are rarely alone for long, as relatives come and go, and sometimes stay for long periods of time. Large family reunions are held during traditional festivals such as Sri Lankan New Year.

Although families are much more scattered that they used to be, there is a preference for living close to, or even with, the husband's family. The wife typically enjoys a good relationship with her own family, and especially relies on her mother for support when her first child is born. Among the rural matrilineal people of the island's east (the majority of whom are Muslim), the husband joins his wife's family instead.

Children move out of the family home only when they get married, though this is changing in more Westernized urban circles. Sri Lankans traditionally have a deep respect for their elders, and parents live with their children once they are unable to support themselves. It is uncommon for anyone to live alone.

The head of the household is traditionally the husband, and in his absence the eldest son assumes this role. However, nearly a quarter of Sri Lankan households today are headed by women in the absence of a suitable man; the tsunami, the ongoing civil conflict, and migration to work abroad are the main contributory factors to this situation.

Although the roles of the sexes in the household are clearly defined, in many cases there is a good deal of equality between the spouses. Women are traditionally responsible for housework, cooking, and raising the children, as well as taking care of the family finances, while the men provide economic stability and represent the family in their public affairs. In agricultural families, women are in charge of weeding and harvesting the crops, while men do the plowing, sowing, and threshing.

Increasingly, husband and wife together make important family decisions, such as the choice of suitable marriage partners for their children. The children traditionally see their father as the role model, while from their mother comes emotional stability and spiritual growth. In urban areas, the frequency of women working has resulted in men becoming more actively involved in the emotional and practical day-to-day aspects of child rearing.

RESPECT FOR ELDERS

Traditionally, socially, and culturally, Sri Lankans have a deep respect for the elderly, both in the home and in public life. Older people are respected as valuable resources with vital skills, experience, and wisdom from which the younger generation is able to benefit when seeking their advice and counsel. They are involved in family-based rituals, and are the custodians and transmitters of cultural traditions. Special emphasis is placed on strengthening the respect of the elderly and their ties with the family during the Sri Lankan New Year festivities.

Religion has also encouraged the social care of the elderly, and in old age parents typically live with their children. Institutional old-age homes do exist in Sri Lanka, but they are not nearly as numerous as in the Western world and are often small and underfunded. Even in the most unavoidable circumstances, when the family is financially unable to look after an elder, or when they are simply unwilling to do so, it is largely seen as a socially unacceptable choice.

THE DAILY ROUTINE
Life in the Village
Rural village life revolves mainly around agriculture. Women generally wake up early to make breakfast for the family, get the children ready for school, and do the household chores. The men go to work in the fields and come home for lunch, which is the main meal of the day. Families usually eat their evening meal together. In many rural households the women also do other work, fitting this around their household duties. The extended family helps with child care.

The pace of life in the village is slow, picking up at harvest time, when there is a great deal of hard work to be done. Settlements are characterized by a place of worship, and religion plays an important role in the daily life of the population. At home, many people light incense and oil candles each morning, and pray at their small Buddhist or Hindu shrines.

Houses in many rural settlements do not have a bathroom but only a simple outside squat toilet. Most water has to be drawn from wells, and where people don't have a well of their own they go to a communal well or tank, or a stream or river, to fetch water and wash. The mornings and evenings are typically when men go to bathe, before and after work, and the middle of the day is generally the time for women and children, who take their laundry and cooking utensils along to wash at the same time.

Mornings in the villages are full of sound, as mobile vendors selling anything from fresh fish to curd melodiously cry their wares, and the ice cream and bread vans play their own special tunes.

Sri Lanka's Tamil plantation workers are among the island's most disadvantaged and isolated groups. In the plantations, the workers typically live on the estates with their families in "line houses" (small adjoining units) located close to the tea fields. Overcrowding is common. Since estate owners are also responsible for providing their workers with social services such as housing, water, and health care, residents are highly dependent upon

them. Schools are often understaffed, and children have few role models outside the plantation industry to gain knowledge of other possible occupations. As a result, many leave school early to go to work and help their families while still remaining dependent on estate life.

Life in the Town

The migration of rural Sri Lankans to the cities is increasingly common. While most leave for urban centers such as Colombo to search for better occupations, only a fortunate few are ever able to secure permanent employment. The ensuing problem of shelter means that many migrants— some of whom are two or three generations away from their rural roots—live in informal and shoddy housing. These include slums and shantytowns located on marginal lands such as canal and railway reservations. New modern housing developments (nearly all of them private) are built away from the congested urban areas and on the outskirts of the cities.

Urban centers such as Colombo demonstrate that modern Sri Lanka is a fusion of old and new. Huge mansions in gated compounds patrolled by security guards are next to poorly built *watte*— wooden planked houses with roofs made from corrugated metal sheets; modern skyscrapers and condominiums overlook canal-side shantytowns; and upscale shopping malls and boutiques stand beside rustic tea shops.

While the majority of city people rely on overcrowded buses to get to work, the privileged few are chauffeured by personal drivers. All, however, have to contend with severe traffic congestion and the resulting pollution.

Sri Lankans prefer to shop for fresh food at individual markets selling fruit, vegetables, meat, fish, and other produce, although many urbanites, especially the Western elite, shop in the large, air-conditioned supermarkets. After work, many urbanites socialize in restaurants, bars, and clubs, and on weekends, bank holidays, and festivals

they take the opportunity to get away from the city and head for the coast.

GROWING UP IN SRI LANKA

In Sri Lanka children are cherished, adored, and indulged. Babies are carried until they can walk, and small children are traditionally kept with their mothers until they are old enough to go to school. The concept of babysitting is almost unheard of, since the extended family provides extensive support. Affluent families have domestic servants and live-in nannies to provide them with child care, taking them away on trips and vacations with them if necessary. While child care facilities in restaurants and such places are uncommon, children are always welcome and allowed to wander around at will. Once the children are past the early years, mothers are typically responsible for the upbringing and discipline of their daughters, as are fathers of their sons.

Where possible, many children attend Montessori or preschool classes before starting their education proper at the age of five years. Three sets of standardized exams from primary level until GCE (Ordinary Level) provide the children with plenty of work both at school and at home. Success in these can lead to subsequent educational privileges, so the children of parents who can afford it often attend private tutorial sessions in the afternoons in addition to their regular schooling. In rural areas where parents are unable to afford transportation, children may walk a few miles to school. Schools are formal: teachers are respected as authority figures, and children wear uniforms.

It is compulsory for children to attend school between the ages of five and thirteen, and after this they are strongly encouraged to stay on until at least the completion of their GCE (Ordinary Level) exams at the age of fifteen or sixteen, after which they can proceed to the higher (Advanced Level) exams to qualify for university entrance. However, since Sri Lankan society is largely agrarian, it is not surprising that more than a third leave at thirteen to help with work in the fields.

University education is free; but competition for the limited number of places means that many qualified students miss out. Those who can't get into one of the sixteen state-funded universities may choose to continue their education abroad, join the Sri Lanka Open University, or enroll in one of the state-owned degree-awarding institutes. Even after this, graduates still have difficulty in finding jobs.

In childhood children learn modesty, self-control, obedience to their parents, and loyalty to their family. Girls and boys mix freely until puberty, and in their teens begin to adopt their adult roles. Girls help with the household chores and learn domestic skills such as cooking. They have much less social freedom than boys, who frequently go out of the house to explore their surroundings and play with friends.

In urban areas and among the Westernized elite boys and girls mix much more freely in their spare time, going shopping and visiting cafés and each other's homes, or going to sports and other clubs.

TV AND THE TELEDRAMA

An increasing number of Sri Lankan households have a television. A range of networks broadcasts a variety of programs, from news and political satires to children's cartoons and films. In the most rural villages, where there may be only a few households with television sets, people crowd the doorways and verandas of their neighbors' houses to watch. Sri Lankan cricket matches, news programs, cultural shows, religious programs, and political satires are especially popular, while the ubiquitous "teledrama" (soaps), both local and Hindi, broadcast every evening, are favorites.

chapter six

TIME OUT

Sri Lankans don't generally go on vacations in the Western sense of the word. Any free time, such as on the occasion of a major religious or cultural event, is taken as an opportunity to go as a group to visit extended family and friends, or with them to attend a family occasion. Vans and buses are hired as they head

for the beaches or hills, temples or pilgrimage sites, historical attractions or wildlife parks, the sound of song and drums typically indicating their arrival long before they come into view.

Sri Lankans will find a way to enjoy themselves wherever they go. In groups they demonstrate a much greater confidence and a more outgoing personality than they do as individuals. While children and teenagers typically have quite a lot of time to themselves, most working adults, especially those living away from home, cherish the occasions when they are able to spend time off with family and friends.

There is plenty to see and do in Sri Lanka, much of it out of doors. Sri Lanka has an abundance of beaches, wildlife parks, rain forests, historic cities, and archaeological sites, as well as many fascinating religious buildings. While Sri Lankans don't generally go trekking or cycling, a number of tour companies offer fascinating trails, which are a perfect way for the foreigner to get off the beaten path and witness authentic Sri Lankan life. Visiting one of the many cultural, historical, and religious attractions at festival times may be crowded and noisy, but is a great way to meet people and immerse oneself in Sri Lankan culture.

SRI LANKANS ON TOUR

When going on a pilgrimage or visiting a temple, Buddhists and Hindus symbolically put coconut palm flowers on the front of their vehicles, while for protection and luck a pendant of lime and chili is attached to the bumper. Both the town of Kataragama—a pilgrimage site for Buddhists, Hindus, and Muslims—and Adam's Peak, or Sri Pada—a holy site for these three faiths and for Christians as well—are the most sacred and popularly visited pilgrimage spots.

Family days out are more common than weeklong stays, while long weekends at the beaches or in the hills are popularly enjoyed by groups of male friends and the mixed Colombo crowd. Structured group tours, predominantly within Sri Lanka but also to India and Thailand, are organized by local temples for a reasonably priced package that includes accommodation—most often in temples. Having an itinerary that takes in the major religious and cultural attractions, these trips most closely resemble a

Western-style package tour, and are popular one-off events for Sri Lankans who can afford it. Since Sri Lankans much prefer the taste—and economies—of home cooking, all of the necessary culinary equipment, including gas stoves, is usually taken with them on their tour. Whether staying with family or in a local guesthouse, the women will set up their own cooking place in the morning to make breakfast for the family and then prepare lunch, which is packed into tiffin carriers (metal lunch boxes) and plastic boxes to be eaten at an attractive stopping point in the journey—often beside a river, a lake, or the sea, to facilitate washing as well as combine with a swim.

TEMPLE ETIQUETTE

While most devout Buddhists will visit their local temple on *poya* days, and take with them offerings of flowers, food, and oil candles, devotees of Buddhism and Hinduism may travel to other important temples or *devalayas* (shrines to particular Hindu gods) further afield to offer worship and say special prayers. The town of Kataragama is the most popular place of veneration. Devotees travel long distances to this sacred place, since it is believed that wishes made and prayers said here have a much higher chance of being answered. All temples welcome visitors, but mosques do not.

Nearly every Buddhist temple has a *dagoba* (white domed structure), a sacred bodhi tree, a Buddha statue, and an image house, where devotees make offerings. The tree is significant, as it was under a bodhi tree that the Buddha gained enlightenment. Devotees light oil lamps, offer flowers (the blooming of a flower upon contact with light is seen as symbolic of the attainment of enlightenment), and circle the tree or

dagoba three times in a clockwise direction. Wishes are written on scraps of material, folded with a coin, and colorfully tied onto the boughs of the bodhi tree in the hope that the wish will come true.

When visiting a temple it is important to keep the impact of your presence to a minimum. Buddha images are considered as sacred as the Buddha himself and, along with monks, are respected accordingly. Buddhist priests have a special place in Buddhist society, being the third of the three elements of veneration—the Buddha (teacher), the Dhamma (teachings), and the Sangha (order of monks).

Visitors, both men and women, should dress modestly at religious sites, covering shoulders and legs. Hats and sunglasses should be removed. When Buddhist and Hindu devotees come to the temple for worship they ritually bathe and then dress in fresh, clean, light-colored clothes. Shoes should always be removed when entering any temple, even a ruined one, as this is considered no less sacred.

SHOPPING FOR PLEASURE

Sri Lanka has a few Western-style department stores and a handful of air-conditioned malls, but these are relatively small and confined to the major cities. The two main shopping malls in Colombo both have food courts, which are frequently populated with groups of young people, shoppers, and office workers taking a break for lunch. In most stores you have to leave your shopping bags in monitored cubbyholes at the entrance. The security guard gives you a tag, which you exchange for your things when you leave.

Most shopping is done in independent retail outlets and markets, where items are usually organized by commodity, so clothes, for example, are found in one region, and electrical items in another. Sri Lanka is famous for its garment exports, and internationally branded goods can be found at very cheap prices. Locally handcrafted items include wooden carvings, baskets, hand-loom textiles, brasses, and silverware.

Sri Lanka can be one of the best places in the world to buy reasonably priced gems, but beware of con artists trying to pass off colored glass. Purchasing from street vendors is a high-risk gamble, and it is best to buy from a government certified store, where guarantees are provided upon purchase. The Sri Lanka Gem and Jewellery Exchange in Colombo will test gems free of charge.

Credit cards are accepted in all major stores and supermarkets, although in some of the smaller shops you may have to pay some commission. For street and market shopping it is best to have cash in small denominations, especially if you are bargaining. Be aware of tour guides pressing you to visit particular shops, as their commission will inflate the final price even more.

Sri Lankan New Year is the most frenzied shopping time, with shoppers hunting for bargains weeks in advance of the big day. The most commonly given presents are clothes and toys, and many street vendors set up special stores for the event and offer tempting discounts as the New Year approaches.

Bargaining

While prices in independent retail shops are fixed, bargaining is essential at street stalls and in markets. Foreigners are often expected to pay a "tourist price" that is much higher than the sum the locals pay. If you are looking for something in particular, do a little research first, and in agreeing on a fair price consider the time and effort that have gone into making the item. Retain a sense of humor and proportion: a small saving for you can be a significant amount to the seller.

A verbal agreement is considered a deal, and it is considered rude if you walk away once you have agreed on a final price.

CULTURAL ACTIVITIES

Music

Sri Lankan music has been influenced by religious chanting, the rhythm of African slave songs, and the melodies, charisma, and commercialization of South Indian (Bollywood) culture. Drums have

been an integral part of Sri Lankan music for centuries, and remain the main rhythm setter today. Other classical Sri Lankan instruments include the *thalampata* (two small cymbals on a string), the reed flute, and the *hakgediya,* or conch shell, which is used to open ceremonies.

The Portuguese and British colonizers brought African slaves (known as *kaffirs,* the Arabic word for "unbelievers") to the island, who introduced a style of music commonly known as the *baila,* characterized by an increasingly frantic, bouncing rhythm. While Western music, especially dance music, has been gaining popularity with the middle and upper classes, *baila* is still the favorite form of pop music throughout Sri Lanka, and is heard frequently in homes and at weddings and parties.

Dance
Sinhalese legend dictates that Sri Lanka's classical dancing originated 2,500 years ago, when a magical dance ritual broke a spell on a bewitched king. Dance is an integral part of the Sri Lankan culture, and is performed on every festive occasion. It is always accompanied by the rhythmic beat of drums, cymbals, and bells. The most prominent styles are the Kandyan (*uda rata natum*) and masked, or low-country (*pahatha rata natum*), dances. Each style differs in the costume, the method of body movement, and rhythm (*tala*), as well as the type of drum used.

Out of the five types of Kandyan dancing, it is the sacred *ves* dance that is most commonly seen at festivals and *peraheras* throughout the island. The *geta bera*, or double-ended drum, typically provides a frenzied beat that encourages the elaborately dressed dancers to leap and flip energetically into the air.

The *yak bera* drum is used in low-country dances such as *kolam* (see Theater, below) and *sunni yakuma* (healing dance ceremony), which both feature elaborately carved masks. These dances often reflect the ancient folk belief-system of Sri Lanka's pre-Buddhist agricultural civilization, when a variety of demons and deities were thought to cause afflictions and diseases. Masks representing the various demons are worn to appease them or scare them away.

Cinema

Not surprisingly, Sri Lanka's cinematic style is similar to that of India, since it has been influenced by Bollywood. Released in 1956, *Rekawa* ("Line of Destiny"), the first feature film by the internationally renowned Sri Lankan director Lester James Peiris, was the first movie to be shot entirely in Sri Lanka. Like Hindi movies, Sri Lankan ones are often love stories, set in rural villages or across ethnic divides, and increasingly relate to the civil war.

Sri Lanka has a modest number of cinemas. However, while they are found only in the major towns and cities of the island, Sri Lankan, Hindi, and Hollywood movies are shown on television and are widely available to rent or buy from VCD and DVD stores. When a new movie comes out, whether in Sinhala, Tamil, or Hindi, huge billboards announce its arrival, and Tamil or Sinhalese subtitles make it accessible to all.

Sri Lankan cinemas typically have three tiers of seating. While seats in the balcony or circle are the most expensive, the experience is the same wherever you sit: frequent chitchat, ringing cell phones, and wolf whistling throughout the movie. Halfway through is an interval, when soft drinks, snacks, and ice creams are sold. The cinema provides an opportunity for amorous Sri Lankan couples to snatch some private time together.

Theater

Theater in Sri Lanka has its origins in the traditional rituals, customs, and folk drama of the nineteenth century. Villagers would get together and act out masked dances (*kolam*) and satirical sketches using familiar characters such as the king, town clerk, policeman, and the farmer and his wife, as well as gods, demons, and animals. By the mid-twentieth century, this ritualistic form of dance drama was to amalgamate with influential Western theater methods to create a new style of modern theater in Sri Lanka. Contemporary Sri Lankan theater has a small following among upper-class urbanites in Colombo.

Plays and comedies by Shakespeare and other famous playwrights are sporadically staged in schools, community centers, and theaters such as the Lionel Wendt, while many of the most recent local productions recount the civil war.

Village communities host their own plays on special occasions, while Christians stage passion plays at Easter. Performed within the Indian Tamil communities of the Hill Country in May, the *Kamenkoothu*—an ancient folk drama telling the story of the Hindu god of love—unites whole villages and lasts for several days.

SPORTS

Sri Lankans have a positive attitude toward sports, and enjoy both playing and watching them. While volleyball is the official national sport, cricket is by far the most popular. Sri Lanka's cricket team gained test status in 1982 and has quickly become one of the best in the world, especially in the one-day match. In 1996 Sri Lanka won the Cricket World Cup, and in 2007 they again reached the final, but were beaten by Australia. Along with India, Pakistan, and Bangladesh, Sri Lanka will be one of the host countries for the 2011 Cricket World Cup.

Evidence of Sri Lanka's love for cricket is everywhere. Children play games on any available patch of land, using whatever they can find in the way of bat and ball. When important international matches are televised, the country virtually grinds to a halt. Fans crowd around every available television and radio set to cheer on their team. Live matches, in one of the many good stadiums island-wide, are characterized by a vocal crowd and a vibrant, carnival-like atmosphere. Players such as the master batsman Sanath Jayasuriya and record-breaking spin bowler Muttiah Muralitharan (Murali) are considered national heroes.

Other popular sports in Sri Lanka are football, swimming, netball, badminton, and athletics. Played in the more famous educational establishments in Colombo, Kandy, and Galle, rugby union has quite a following. The Singer Sri Lankan Airlines Rugby 7s is a major annual tournament held in Kandy and attended by every rugby-playing nation in Asia.

Sri Lanka has its own version of baseball called *elle* (pronounced el-lay). While the gist of the game is similar, in *elle* the ball is smaller and the bat is replaced by a long bamboo stick. *Elle* is played in schools and in communities at festive periods, especially Sri Lankan New Year.

EATING OUT
Sri Lankan Cuisine
Sri Lankan cuisine is fierier than its Indian neighbor. Fresh chilies or chili powder are liberally added to most curries—generally, the darker the gravy, the more intense the heat. Rice is the main staple food and is eaten in one form or another at all meals; string hoppers (steamed vermicelli-like nests), plain hoppers (crispy bowl-shaped pancakes), and *pittu* are all made from rice flour. Fiery *sambols* of coconut, tomato, onion, chili, and dried Maldive fish

typically act as flavor enhancers. Most curries are cooked in oil (coconut or vegetable) and may contain coconut milk, but Sri Lankan food is relatively healthy, and the wide variety of pulses, lentils, and fresh vegetables used make it an ideal cuisine for vegetarians.

Sri Lanka has an abundance of tropical fruits, and so it is not surprising that the most common dessert—or breakfast—is either a fruit platter or a deliciously sweet fruit salad. Fresh juices are available everywhere, alongside a limited selection of soft drinks and bottled water. Buffalo curd is blended into the drink *lassi*, or served with rich kithul palm honey as a traditional dessert.

Restaurants
Sri Lanka has a wide variety of eating establishments, ranging from the most basic rice and curry *kades* (shops) and bakeries serving "short eats" (buns, pastries, and *roti* bread) in nearly every village and town to the exclusive,

air-conditioned restaurants serving international cuisine in Colombo and top hotels island-wide. Mid-range restaurants are abundant in towns and tourist resorts, where the menus will feature a large selection of Eastern and Western dishes including plenty of fish, seafood, and sometimes beef and pork. Fish fresh from the Indian Ocean is preferred over the softer, less tasty river fish. Muslim establishments only sell *halal* meat and never pork. Remember the dietary rules when ordering, or when picking a restaurant in which to meet a Muslim friend.

Kades sell Sri Lankan food and rarely have a menu; expect rice and curry for lunch, hoppers and sambol for dinner, and sweet Ceylon tea. Tea is served at any time of the day with or without milk and normally with lots of sugar unless you request otherwise. While Sri Lankans traditionally eat with their fingers, cutlery is always available if you ask. Rice and curry in local *kades* can often be far better and much more authentic than you would find in a five-star hotel. Those located on main thoroughfares see a large quantity of customers on a daily basis, which ensures that the food is very fresh. Don't be put off by the gloomy, messy appearance of some *kades*, as most are quick, tasty, clean, and very good value.

Local restaurants in the cities and along the roadsides are efficient and well patronized by travelers, office workers, and commuters. Most menus feature a range of dishes such as fried rice, noodles, *chop suey* (a Chinese dish), and deviled meats. While in many cases the food is good, Sri Lankans will still agree that it is not comparable with what they get at home!

Fast-food chains are found mainly in Colombo, and most offer home delivery. Food courts with a selection of world cuisine are found in some of the city's larger shopping malls and are well patronized throughout the day. Lunch packets are probably the island's cheapest and most well-known take-out option: a portion of rice and a variety of curries are wrapped up in plastic sheets, parceled up in newspaper, and sold in *kades* or on the street.

If you have invited Sri Lankan friends out for dinner, it is customary for you to pay the bill. If they have invited you, it is polite for you to offer to pay, though you may be refused. If you are hosted for dinner in a restaurant, it is polite to return the invitation at some point in the near future.

TIPPING

Tipping is expected in Sri Lanka, since wages are low. While most restaurants and some hotels include a 10 percent service charge on the bill, Sri Lankans might also leave a further 10 percent tip on top of this. Tipping is a way of showing your appreciation and understanding of the realities of life for the workers. Wealthier Sri Lankans may tip more frequently—to a shop assistant who carries their bags to their car; to someone who finds and saves them a seat on a busy bus or train; and to a doorman who runs an errand for them. It is customary to tip housekeepers and bellboys, and taxi or three-wheeler drivers if they have given you good service. Stick to small tips rather than large sums of money.

NIGHTLIFE

In the cities the nightlife is varied, offering something for everyone. There are restaurants and possibly bars in every town but, since only the most Westernized women drink, the local bars tend to be dingy and male-oriented. Many men prefer to purchase alcohol more cheaply in a liquor store and drink somewhere else with their friends. Rural Sri Lankans rise at the crack of dawn to start work, and it's the urbanites who are more likely to stay out until the early hours of the morning.

The southwestern coastal areas cater to the tourist trade with beach bars and restaurants. In Colombo, an increasing range of pubs, bars, and clubs offer Western-style entertainment, including live bands, big-screen international sports fixtures, and karaoke. Party planners and disc jockeys arrange frequent glitzy club nights in or outside the city, which are well attended by the Colombo crowd. Colombo has a few casinos.

Imported spirits are available in the larger hotels and restaurants, but they are expensive. Most Sri Lankans drink the national beverage, *arrack*—distilled from the sap of coconut palm flowers—or one of the many local varieties of vodka, gin, and rum. Beer has been produced locally since the nineteenth century, and remains popular. The local brand is Lion, and Carlsberg is also often available. They are most commonly sold in reusable bottles that hold 625 ml (just over one and a third pints).

chapter seven

TRAVEL, HEALTH, & SAFETY

Sri Lanka has a wealth of beautiful beaches, archaeological attractions, and national parks full of wildlife to delight the foreign visitor. While there are many modes of transportation to reach them, long journeys on congested, poorly surfaced roads call for a lot of patience. Travelers should be very aware of road etiquette, whether they are driving, cycling, or on foot.

Travel in Sri Lanka is a multisensory experience of sound and spectacle. Buses and trains are often

overcrowded, so expect impromptu musical performances, food vendors, delays, and sweaty journeys with lots of social interaction. Taxis allow for relative peace and privacy.

Compared to the rest of Asia, standards of hygiene in Sri Lanka are reasonable, and the country has a good health care system. It is also one of the safest and easiest places in the region for women to travel alone, provided they act responsibly and take sensible precautions.

ROADS AND TRAFFIC
Driving
Foreign visitors wishing to drive in Sri Lanka
should do so with confidence and not be
intimidated by other drivers. Temporary one-
month government driving permits can be issued
on production of a valid international driver's
license. Driving is on the left and the minimum
driving age is eighteen.

Traveling by road is a frustrating experience,
since, despite Sri Lanka's modest size, navigating
the heavily congested roads contributes
to achingly long
journey times.
The ninety-mile
(146-km) journey
from Colombo to
Matara takes an
exhausting four
hours by car. The
most important

highways linking the capital to significant towns
and cities have recently been resurfaced, while
work is under way on the Southern Lanka Express
Highway that will connect Colombo to Galle and
Matara and cut journey times down to an
estimated one and a half and two hours
respectively. It is due to be completed in 2010.

For the foreign visitor the experience of
driving, or even being driven, on Sri Lanka's
chaotic roads can be alarming. Urban centers and
busily congested highways where the more

forceful vehicles, such as buses and trucks, assert their domineering might over softer road users, such as motorcycles, bicycles, and bullock carts, are not for the fainthearted. However, despite the chaos there is a method to this madness, and a large amount of the weaving, light flashing, and honking is an organized art form that new drivers will soon get to learn. This is no place for timid drivers; assertiveness is the key.

While there are rules for driving in Sri Lanka, most are disregarded and few are ever enforced.

Instead Sri Lankans follow a secret highway code that affords the biggest vehicles supreme right of way as buses aggressively tailgate and honk at anything smaller in their path. Typical Western forms of driver communication are reversed, so that flashing your headlights at an oncoming vehicle does not mean you are giving way but that you are demanding that the other vehicle do so. Sri Lankan drivers are some of the most horn-happy in the world, and use of the horn has different meanings depending on length and intensity. They are also incredibly impatient, so passing one or two cars at a time on blind curves and at junctions is not uncommon.

Only the larger cities have traffic lights, and these are grudgingly obeyed, especially if there is a traffic policeman present. Traffic circles can often be a free-for-all: although vehicles already on the circle have legal priority, others push on if they feel they have been waiting long enough. Lane discipline is almost nonexistent, and often where there are only two lanes marked on the road vehicles line up at least four strong. There is no concept of a slow lane or a passing lane, both being used for the same end!

The number of traffic policemen on the main roads is increasing, and they frequently stop drivers for speeding and other traffic offenses. In built-up areas the speed limit is 56 kmph (35 mph) and outside towns it is 75 kmph (45 mph). Oncoming vehicles often warn each other of the presence of policemen by flashing their lights. If a driver is penalized for a driving offense, including talking on a cell phone, their driver's license is confiscated and taken to the nearest police station. Irrespective of the driver's residence, he must go there to pay the fine and reclaim his license. Drunk driving is illegal, and if caught the driver is taken into police custody. Penalties range from a loss of license and insurance to a spell in prison if the driver has caused a fatal accident.

While a large majority of Sri Lankan roads are poorly lit, dangerously potholed, and badly signposted, there are other major hazards: cumbersome cattle, suicidal dogs, pedestrians and cyclists seemingly unaware of the road around them, speeding three-wheelers, slow bullock carts, and strange-looking "land masters"—small, belt-driven diesel motors pulling a trailer. The latter two are common forms of transportation in the most rural areas, where other transport services are lacking.

Drivers go through a ritual of circling the wheel with their hands three times and saying a quick prayer before setting off on a long journey, and deposit a few coins in the till when they pass a Buddhist temple, in the belief that they are gaining protection from the Buddha. They also adorn their vehicles with religious talismans that they trust will ensure them a safe journey.

Checkpoints

As a result of the civil conflict, security checkpoints are a way of life, and there are many along most main roads. While drivers must carry with them proof of their identity, vehicle registration papers, and insurance details at all times, passengers must also be prepared to show officers and army personnel some form of identification. While this may be time-consuming, it is a necessary procedure to ensure everyone's safety.

Accidents

Road accidents are common in Sri Lanka and, while most are minor incidents, there are many that end in tragedy. When an accident occurs, onlookers typically crowd around, making unhelpful comments as they survey the damage. Any victims are quickly rushed to the hospital, and chalk is used to mark their positions on the road, as well as the position of the involved vehicles' tires so that they can be moved out of the way if possible. In the meantime the police are called.

If the scrape is minor, the drivers will usually get out and exchange a few cross words before continuing on their journey If there is significant damage but no injury, then the cost is either settled through insurance or, if the drivers are not in possession of insurance, worked out between themselves. The increasing number of traffic policemen and checkpoints on the roads has successfully forced most Sri Lankans to buy car insurance of some kind. Only drivers without full insurance (where the companies send on-the-spot representatives to survey the damage) need a police report to make an insurance claim.

Bikes and Motorbikes

Bicycles are one of the popular forms of transport, and it is very common to see two or even three people squeezed on to one bike. Cycling is ideal for the quieter rural roads; however on the main roads cyclists are much more vulnerable to the might of the buses and trucks that are in no way sensitive to their presence. While the side of the main road to the left of either a white or yellow line is designated for cyclists, other road users rarely recognize this, so caution should be exercised at all times.

Motorbikes are also very common in Sri Lanka, and are preferred for their ability to weave quickly in and out of traffic. They are also a more affordable option than a car and used to transport the family about even if that means there are as many as four or five passengers, including children and babies, on board.

Pedestrians

While sidewalks do exist in the towns and cities, most are badly constructed and incomplete. Blocked drains result in unpleasant flooding, while cars and rubbish dumped on the pavements force pedestrians to walk on the roads even though there is a raging torrent of traffic around them. Pedestrians must always remain aware, and be prepared to get out of the way fast if need be.

Yellow and white pedestrian crossings are found everywhere, especially in urban areas and near schools. While the right of way is supposed to belong to the pedestrian, this is rarely the case as most drivers stop only if they see that someone is already halfway across. When crossing the road you must be bold but sensible; don't cross on a blind curve, and don't rely on your right of way at pedestrian crossings.

Parking

Sri Lankans consider that any large enough space is good enough to park in. However, on main roads in cities—especially Colombo—it is often very difficult to find a legal parking place, and the situation is made worse by current high-security practices in the capital, where cars are filtered along one-way roads and encouraged to keep moving.

A yellow or white line marked on the road designates an area for cyclists, and/or pedestrians if there is no curb. If the line is yellow, parking is not permitted. If the line is white, you may park, but the vehicle must be completely to the left of the line. Main roads in urban areas are off-limits for parking (though signs telling you this are sporadic) and public car parks are rare, other than at the larger city malls. Vehicles may be towed away if they are found in a no parking zone, and penalties are issued to drivers. Parking in front of government and military buildings and embassies is forbidden.

If you are visiting a hotel, restaurant, city mall, or even an independent retailer with a car park, there is usually an attendant, smartly dressed in green, who is responsible for the organization of vehicles. He will direct you into a spot and assist you when backing on to the main road on your departure.

LOCAL TRANSPORTATION

The majority of Sri Lankans rely on public transportation, which extensively links even the smallest and most remote rural villages throughout the island. Even those who own motorbikes will take advantage of the many bus routes and more limited train destinations when going on a long journey. Each mode of transport offers a unique flavor, and can be enjoyed more or less comfortably, depending on the price.

Buses

Buses are the staple form of public transportation in Sri Lanka, and are commonly crowded. There are two types of bus. The government, or CTB (Central Transport Board), buses are cumbersome Tata vehicles, dark red or yellow, in various states of disrepair; private buses are either large, white-stickered Ashok Leylands or smaller, Japanese, air-conditioned, intercity minibuses.

Intercity buses are generally the fastest, since they have limited stops. Apart from the long-distance services, buses rarely follow a structured timetable, but residents know that local buses pass with relative frequency. Traveling by bus is generally a hot and sweaty affair, especially if it is overcrowded. Highly decorated interiors feature electric Buddha images and other religious paraphernalia, while Sinhala music often blares loudly from the speakers. The front seats behind the driver are always reserved for the clergy, so if a monk boards anyone sitting there must move. The ones immediately behind these are reserved for pregnant women, and should also be given up if needed. Even in the most crowded situations the conductor will wind his way through the passengers to sell you your ticket.

Taxis

There are a few types of taxi in Sri Lanka, the most characteristic being the ubiquitous motorized three-wheelers, or trishaws. Metered taxis can be found in Colombo, and are efficient and relatively good value. For longer journeys hiring a car—usually an air-conditioned van— and driver is a good way to travel since most hotels and guesthouses accommodate drivers who are bringing guests. Drivers in Colombo and the main tourist resorts typically have a good command of English.

Three-wheelers, which will give you your most characteristic and memorable ride in Sri Lanka, are ideal for short trips and are found in abundance throughout the island. Some are basic; others, decked out with glittering accessories, booming stereos, and decorated interiors, are a great source of pride to their owners. Prices are not fixed, and passengers should agree on a fare, based on the distance and time, before embarking on a trip. Bargaining is expected.

Trains

Traveling by train is often a less stressful experience than by bus and, in most cases, even cheaper. All major routes radiate from Colombo, most of them constructed by the British in the late nineteenth and early twentieth centuries to facilitate the movement of trade and plantation crops. If not overcrowded, trains are a very pleasant way to explore the island, especially the Hill Country.

On trains there are three classes, with first class available only on selected journeys. A few long-distance trains have sleeper carriages. In most cases trains are slower and more prone to delays than buses, but often give the visitor a more enriching cultural experience, with food vendors, beggars singing haunting tunes, and groups of friends dancing in the aisles to the rhythm of a drum. Trains are also where Sri Lankans have the best opportunity to engage you in conversation, and a friendly chat may even lead to an invitation to a Sri Lankan home!

Air

Sri Lanka has one well-serviced international airport at Katanayake, and domestic airports at

Ratmalana and Jaffna. The A9 road between Colombo and Jaffna is, at the time of writing, closed due to the ongoing conflict, and traveling by air is currently the only way to reach Jaffna. Even in times of peace it is by far the quickest and most comfortable.

There is also an island-wide air taxi service operated by Sri Lankan Airlines, and also the option of traveling by helicopter with Deccan Aviation.

WHERE TO STAY

Sri Lanka has a well-developed tourist industry with a great range of accommodation to suit every budget, especially in the most popular resort destinations. While prices in the most exclusive hotels and villas are not usually subject to change, it is possible to negotiate a lower price in most other hotels and guesthouses, especially from May to October, the low season for tourism, when prices may be reduced to half their high-season rates.

HEALTH

While it is advisable to start planning the health aspects of your trip well in advance of your departure, it is reassuring to know that most places are free from malaria, including Colombo, the southwest coast, and the Hill Country. However, since mosquitoes carry other diseases such as dengue fever, Japanese encephalitis and, more recently, chikungunya, it is important to avoid being bitten. Common precautions include wearing light-colored clothing with long sleeves at night, using a repellent containing deet, and sleeping under a net.

Make sure you are up-to-date with standard vaccinations such as tetanus, polio, hepatitis A, and diphtheria. If you are staying in Sri Lanka for a long period of time, you might also consider being inoculated against typhoid and rabies. Travel insurance is essential. Keep any hospital or medical receipts so that you can be reimbursed later.

Standards of hygiene in Sri Lanka are good compared to the rest of Asia and even though diarrhea is the most common traveler's complaint there, it doesn't compare to India's notorious "Delhi belly." Preventive measures include drinking only bottled water, avoiding ice, washing salads in purified water, and avoiding undercooked meat and fish. Stick to freshly cooked, hot food, and avoid anything that looks as if it has been sitting out for a while. As a general rule, the busier the establishment, the better!

Medical care in Sri Lanka is reasonably good. Many doctors have been trained in the West, giving them a good command of English. A free health care system is in place; however, as this is at the discretion of each doctor, foreigners might (and often do) have to pay. There is also private health care. The facilities and service in the bigger private hospitals in Colombo are first class, although many of the local government hospitals suffer from understaffing and overcrowding. For nonemergencies, family doctors and pharmacies can be found in every town. Appointments are necessary only if you are attending a private hospital or doctor.

SAFETY AND SECURITY
Terrorism
Sri Lanka has been fighting a civil war for over thirty years. Security is tight in most urban areas, especially Colombo, and armed checkpoints, manned by both the police and the army, are common island-wide. While fighting between government forces and the LTTE takes place in the north and east of the country, the conflict has affected other parts of the island minimally, especially the south. The conflict is a political one arising from ethnic tensions, and foreign nationals are not seen as targets.

Suicide bombs are a characteristic of the war; while the LTTE primarily aims at military or political targets, sporadic bus and train bombs aimed at killing civilians have also occurred on occasion in Colombo. Security on public transportation has been stepped up and in many checkpoints bus passengers have to get off to allow the vehicle to be searched. In conflict zones, there is a danger of mines if you step off the main road.

It is always advisable to check with your foreign office for the most up-to-date safety advice prior to your arrival in Sri Lanka.

Crime
Despite this, traveling in Sri Lanka is remarkably safe. Muggings are not common, and violent crime against foreigners is almost unheard of. Petty theft is not as rife as in the rest of Asia, but visitors should always take sensible precautions and look after their belongings, especially on crowded buses and trains. Thefts in hotels and guesthouses occasionally occur, so if there is a safe available then it is better to use it.

Sri Lanka is well known for its con artists. Scams and touting are widespread in a few tourist areas, most notably Colombo's Galle Face Green. Be cautious when approached by "charity collectors," who may be fakes, by anyone selling gems on the street, and by three-wheeler drivers offering to take you to nonexistent elephant festivals. Those who tirelessly attempt to prove their trustworthiness to you should probably be politely avoided.

Women

Sri Lanka is a conservative society, where women are judged by the way they dress and behave. As a rule, the more modestly you dress, and the better you blend in, the less unwanted attention you will receive. Staring is common, and in most cases represents nothing more harmful than curiosity.

Sri Lanka is considered to be one of the safer places for women to travel alone in Asia, and in general men are courteous. However, you should always take sensible precautions: don't go anywhere unlit at night, and especially not with a stranger. If you are verbally harassed on the street, or when exploring isolated places, it is best to avoid eye contact and walk away. Anger is not a solution, since it is likely to provoke the harassers more.

Sexual harassment has been known to happen on trains and buses under cover of overcrowding. Women should beware of stray hands, and politely ignore any unwanted verbal attention. If a man does make an attempt at molestation, draw the attention of other passengers to the person responsible. While passengers can't be relied upon to do anything to assist in this type of situation, letting others know what is happening is usually enough to embarrass and scare off the molester. In such cases it is not only foreign women who are targets, but Sri Lankan women too.

chapter eight

BUSINESS BRIEFING

The rich diversity of Sri Lanka is well represented in its business landscape. Small- and medium-sized enterprises (SMEs) make up the bulk of its commercial concerns, alongside government-owned institutions and an increasing number of multinationals. Sri Lanka has been transformed from a statist to a market-oriented economy over the last few decades, with attractive benefits for foreign investors; however the civil war continues to cast a dark shadow over the business environment as a whole.

While there are many advantages to doing business in Sri Lanka—the island's multiskilled and multilingual labor force are certainly an asset to the country—high taxes, coupled with rigid labor laws that make it almost impossible to fire anyone, are the downsides. While the time taken to set up a business in Sri Lanka has decreased in recent years, the issuing of permits and licenses, especially in construction, are bound by a lot of red tape, making the process costly and frustratingly lengthy.

The most common Sri Lankan enterprises— public and private limited liability companies—are still the most suitable for foreign investors, along with joint ventures. Representative or liaison offices may also be set up. Investors should remember that the continuing conflict has the potential to affect the economic situation. Sri Lanka has a Free Trade Agreement with India and Pakistan.

Registering a business with the Board of Investment (BOI) can result in generous tax breaks and other entitlements. A local partner is not a legal requirement, but it is an advantage to have one, in whom you have trust, as he or she will have inside knowledge of the market and of commercial law, and be able to cut through the red tape, saving you much time and trouble.

The major cities have good facilities in the larger hotels where business centers are equipped with Wi-Fi or broadband Internet connections, faxes, printing facilities, satellite television, and in some cases audiovisual equipment. The pace of business is slower and more relaxed than in Western countries.

The offices of private businesses are usually open from Monday to Friday from 8:30 a.m. until

5:00 p.m.; some also work until 1:00 p.m. on
Saturdays. Smaller businesses might open earlier
or finish at a later time of 6:00 p.m., and a few
have introduced more flexible working hours, to
make it easier for staff to attend to their own
personal business and potentially avoid lengthy
delays in getting to and from work. Government
offices are open only during the week. Muslim
businesses may be closed on Fridays between
12 noon and 2:00 p.m. for their weekly prayer
session (*Salat-al-Jummah*).

THE BUSINESS CULTURE

Regionalism, religion, language, and caste are
factors to be aware of when doing business in Sri
Lanka, as these will all shape behavioral patterns.
In general, all ethnic groups mix and observe
harmony in the workplace. Etiquette and
approach may need to be modified depending on
whom you are addressing and the circumstances.
Humor is appreciated, and if used in moderation
shows you to be friendly and approachable;
however you must be careful not to offend certain
groups of people.

People in larger companies will have a good
command of English, but if you are dealing with
smaller companies and government departments
it may be wise to secure a translator or a trusted
third party for both verbal and written
communications.

The Importance of Personal Relationships

As is common throughout Asia, the building of long-lasting relationships is the key to business success in Sri Lanka. Sri Lankans like to feel at ease, so it is important to invest time in building a relationship. First impressions are very important, and honesty is highly valued. Trust is also vital, especially because the legal framework of the country cannot always be relied upon to bail you out of a situation, even when there are contracts involved. While trust takes time to earn, a solid grounding results in prompt payments, reliable communication, and a general ease in business partnership. Openness, warmth, respect for the culture, and an ability to fit in are important qualities for the foreign businessman. Patience is most definitely a virtue.

Contacts

Knowing the right people is very important, and good contacts play a vital role in getting things done. Sometimes the status of a worker's family, their education, connections, or degrees from abroad may be considered more important than their ability to lead, their skills, and dedication. Family businessmen have been known to favor family allegiance and loyalty over competitive skills, and to give young, inexperienced family members prominent roles. Sri Lankans often face pressure from extended family and friends hoping to gain favors from their contacts. Social gain is a strong motivator.

Hierarchy

Not surprisingly, given the
traditional social order of the country,
hierarchy plays a fundamental role in
Sri Lankan business culture, where the
boss is very much the boss. Decisions
can sometimes be painfully slow in
coming, especially in government sector
institutions, since they are always referred to and
made at the highest level. The more junior your
contact, the longer decisions will take to happen.
In many cases initial meetings will take place with
middle-ranking personnel, who gather
information to pass on to the decision makers.

Nonconfrontation

Understanding the Sri Lankan communication
style is vital for carrying out business. Sri Lankans
are nonconfrontational, so harmony should be
maintained even when things go wrong. Public
displays of emotion are uncommon and a display
of impatience, frustration, and annoyance will
never work in your favor. As we have seen, "face" is
very important throughout Asia, and as pride can
sometimes come before business, putting people
in awkward positions or under pressure can result
in failure. Disagreements can be acerbic and can
lead to frustrating and vindictive conduct.

Directness is not common among Sri Lankans.
People have an aversion to saying "no," because of
the possibility of causing disappointment or
offense, so be aware that noncommittal answers,

long pauses, and evasive tactics are very likely to reflect a negative opinion. Most communication goes on between the words rather than within them so you must learn to be intuitive. However frustrating this may be, you should understand that you might not be told directly how others feel or exactly what they want.

BUSINESS ETIQUETTE

First impressions are important, and showing an understanding of Sri Lankan business etiquette is an ideal opportunity to boost your positive image.

Business Dress

Owing to the hot and humid climate, business attire in Sri Lanka is less formal than in the West. While dress codes will vary according to the formality of the business sector, it is important to show respect for your contacts by always being smart—but not in a way that reflects negatively on anyone else. On formal occasions, such as when visiting high government officials and at first meetings, men should wear a lightweight suit; long-sleeved shirts, ties, and pressed trousers are acceptable in more casual situations. Women should always dress modestly and avoid sleeveless blouses, short skirts, and low necklines. Jewelry should be simple and discreet.

Timekeeping

It is important to observe punctuality in keeping business appointments, as this is also regarded as a sign of respect. You are expected to be on time. Lateness by more than half an hour on the part of Sri Lankans is rare—except when meeting with government officials or functionaries, when you should expect to wait. If you think you might be late, it is considered polite to call and notify your contact. If it is necessary to cancel a meeting, this should be done at the earliest possible opportunity.

When you are planning your schedule, leave at least an hour between appointments in case of late starts or meetings that run longer than expected. Travel in Sri Lanka, especially in Colombo, can be hectic and congested, and so you should leave even more time between meetings if you have some distance to go. It is realistic to plan to attend no more than three fixed appointments in one day.

Schedules are more relaxed than in the West, as it is generally accepted that things in Sri Lanka take longer to accomplish. It's best not to expect Sri Lankan companies to meet your production or service deadlines, especially when dealing with government institutions, but close contact and direct communication with your Sri Lankan counterparts can assist in speeding up the process. It is also important to take the country's many public holidays into account when making your business plans.

Business Cards

Business cards are essential, and are usually exchanged after an initial handshake and formal greeting. They should be presented and received with both hands and studied for a few seconds before being carefully put away. It is important to treat business cards with respect—stuffing them quickly into a pocket is considered highly disrespectful.

Titles and qualifications are considered important, so these should be added to your business card. Having one side of your card translated into either Sinhala or Tamil is a nice touch but is not essential. It is very cheap to have good cards printed in Sri Lanka.

Gift Giving

Business gifts are acceptable in Sri Lanka, but should never be offered at the first meeting. Wait for a special occasion, such as the confirmation of a business deal or the completion of a project. Don't be extravagant, or the gift could be misconstrued as a bribe or unfairly pressure the recipient into returning a gift of the same value. Choose something modest—a souvenir of your home country, elegant stationery, an attractive calendar, or something that your company manufactures.

MEETINGS

Appointments should be made in a timely fashion and confirmed closer to the day. It is always good practice to send some background information on your company, the names of those who will be attending, and an outline of the agenda for your meeting in advance. First meetings tend to be the most formal occasions, and smart dress is appropriate.

On entering the room you should greet the most senior figure first as a mark of respect by shaking hands. Men should wait for a woman to extend her hand first. Use formal forms of address—titles are important to Sri Lankans—and don't use first names until you are invited to. If your contact has no professional title, just use Mr., Mrs., or Miss with the person's first name or surname.

Since good business relationships are key in Sri Lanka, it is important to introduce yourself and engage in some polite conversation at the start of meetings. You should expect a lot of small talk before business is discussed; use this time to get to know your contacts. Good topics to discuss are family, your country, cricket, and your impressions of Sri Lanka. If you have met your contact before you could ask after his or her family. Both men and women are equally open to conversation.

Small talk has its advantages; since Sri Lankan contract law can be rather sketchy, personal rather than contractual relationships are often what bind businesses together. Sri Lankans feeling comfortable with you on a personal level will result in a well-grounded and long-lasting business relationship even in times of trouble.

The decision makers do not always attend meetings. Initial meetings will typically be attended by middle-ranking personnel, who will collate the information to pass on to the decision maker. Their opinion is important, as they will be the ones representing you to the higher authorities, and so making a good first impression is vital. Business in Sri Lanka is hierarchically organized, and only business counterparts of equal rank address each other in meetings.

Meetings can go on for a couple of hours, and you can expect to be served lots of highly sweetened tea along with cookies or sweets. Don't be put off if your meeting is interrupted by other business, or if someone is called to the telephone, as this sometimes has to happen and should not be interpreted as rude. Always remain polite and friendly throughout.

It is very important to follow up your meeting with telephone calls to sustain the relationships that were forged and check that the business is going ahead as discussed.

PRESENTATIONS

Presentations are increasingly common in Sri Lanka, and technical equipment is now quite sophisticated. Certainly the business premises in many of the island's top hotels are first class.

Presentations are conducted in much the same way as in the West, although they have a higher chance of being interrupted.

In presenting your ideas, it is important to have a relaxed and friendly approach. Explain, as clearly as you can, your vision, and how you plan to achieve your goals. Clarity at this stage will help to avoid misunderstandings and will make the later part of your job easier.

Presentations should always be concise and easily understandable, as Sri Lankans will be put off by overly complex or unnecessarily vague information. Since the decision maker may not be present, you want to make sure that your Sri Lankan counterpart is able to relay your vision and goals clearly to the higher authorities. When dealing with smaller companies and government institutions, it always helps to have some presentation materials, and perhaps the main points, translated into either Sinhalese or Tamil for local consumption.

It is recommended that you bring your own laptop with you, but other equipment should be provided. Calling in advance to find out what equipment is available is advisable if you are planning on giving a particularly technical display. Presentations depend on the nature of the topic discussed but do not typically exceed one hour. Remember that the level of seniority of the person you are presenting to gives an indication of the time that you have; people in authority tend to have less time, so concentrate on getting to the point quickly. If there are interruptions, wait until you have their full attention again before continuing.

NEGOTIATIONS

In negotiations, remember that Sri Lankans are not direct in their demands and that they don't like saying the word "no." Vague and noncommittal comments often hint at a negative response. It is important to learn to read between the lines.

You should be clear from the start about your aims, requirements, expectations, and conditions. Take minutes or document every discussion and agreement for future reference. Negotiations can be slow, especially in the early stages and if you have to do the groundwork with middle managers. You'll only be able to seal the deal with the decision makers, so try to get to meet them face-to-face if you can, to discuss your aims and concerns directly.

When negotiating with Sri Lankans, avoid high-pressure tactics. Being confrontational or forceful will have a negative effect, while criticisms and disagreements should only be voiced in the most diplomatic manner. Politeness is the key to clinching deals.

Business decisions may be based as much on faith, intuition, and feeling as on statistical data. Sinhalese and Tamil people believe in astrology, and are guided by their belief in a higher force that controls most aspects of day-to-day life. Astrologers may be consulted to gain clearance for new business premises or to establish a good or auspicious time to start a new project. Many firmly believe that any outcome, good or bad, is a result of *karma*. It is wise to respect these cultural values, and not show any frustration if they cause delays. If the negotiating process is successful, and you have a deal, it is appropriate to acknowledge this with a celebratory dinner, drink, or gift.

CONTRACTS

Sri Lankan commercial law is largely statutory. While it was codified before independence in 1948 and still reflects many aspects of the British law of the time, amendments have mostly kept pace with successive legal changes in the UK. The Board of Investment Law, the Intellectual Property Act, the Companies Act, and the Consumer Affairs Authority Act are just some of the important legal enactments that regulate Sri Lankan commercial affairs. Civil law is predominantly Roman-Dutch.

A contract will give your deal legality in Sri Lanka, but unfortunately, if things do go wrong, the court system cannot be always relied upon. Resolving disputes in the courts is time-consuming, since procedures allow for one party to prolong the case indefinitely. Many companies prefer to resolve disputes out of court and include an arbitration clause in their contracts. In any case it is important to be represented by a good legal team.

Contracts are presented in either English or Sinhalese, and while it is very important that you instruct your lawyer to check a contract before you sign it, the lawyer does not need to be present when you do so. You are expected to honor the terms of a contract once they are agreed on, and you should make frequent follow-up calls to ensure proper compliance.

DEALING WITH THE GOVERNMENT

The government exercises a great deal of control over businesses in Sri Lanka, and many administrative appointments are politically motivated. Having the right contacts politically— the higher the better—is a significant advantage. The Board of Investment (BOI) is a government institution specifically set up as a one-stop shop for potential and current foreign investors.

A bureaucratic and onerous tax system combined with rigid labor laws weighs heavily on all businesses operating in Sri Lanka. The tax system is considered a major constraint, and the difficulty in complying with it has created an environment conducive to corruption. The island ranks well below other South Asian countries on the ease of paying taxes, making it less competitive in attracting investment. While the Sri Lankan authorities have begun to simplify procedures by reducing the number of tariffs, companies still have to spend a great deal of time with tax officials, make many payments a year, and forfeit a large percentage of their profits. The result is significant tax evasion.

CORRUPTION

Sri Lanka has its fair share of corruption problems. High-level corruption, characterized by cronyism, is frequently discussed in the Sri Lankan media; however, there have never been any major cases resulting in a conviction. Corruption in Sri Lanka is still at a moderate level compared to other Asian countries (ranking just below India and above Pakistan and Bangladesh in Transparency International's Corruption Perception Index); however it is still identified by many companies as one of the major constraints on business operations, especially by investors in large projects and companies seeking government procurement contracts.

Bribery is common in Sri Lanka, so companies operating businesses there risk encountering corrupt practices. Investors should exercise caution when seeking local persons to facilitate business transactions on their behalf, to avoid recruiting potentially corrupt agents. A Bribery Commission investigates charges of corruption.

The public sector is perceived to be the most corrupt sphere, where bribes are offered to obtain necessary permits and licenses. Those working in this sector consider their salaries to be low and regard bribes as a way of supplementing incomes. Loopholes in the law are also a contributory factor. However, despite the fact that it's common practice, there are many employees who would be deeply offended if they were to be offered a bribe.

WOMEN IN BUSINESS

Sri Lankan businesspeople are accustomed to dealing with foreign women in managerial positions, even though there are relatively few Sri Lankan women in similar positions. Gender equality is enshrined in Sri Lankan law, and women are treated equally in the workplace. Those at the higher levels can expect to receive the same amount of respect as their male counterparts, especially in the corporate and private sector.

The first country in the world to have a female prime minister, Sri Lanka set the standard to some extent, and women are taking on more authoritative roles; however it is still much more common for a man to be the decision maker in a large company.

SOCIALIZING

Entertaining in a business context, while important, is quite modest in Sri Lanka. Sri Lankans are very hospitable, and many enjoy getting out of the office to talk business in a less formal setting. Unless you know your hosts quite well, it is unlikely that you will be invited to their home. An invitation to a business associate's home, therefore, is a clear sign of acceptance, and should not be refused.

Socializing mainly takes place in social clubs, restaurants, and bars, some of which are located in Colombo's more prestigious five-star hotels. It

is unlikely that spouses will join you for a business lunch or dinner. Remember that many women in Sri Lanka refrain from drinking alcohol, so if there are to be women in the group it is advisable to choose a café or a restaurant rather than a bar as a meeting place, so as not to put them in an uncomfortable situation.

Similarly, be aware of a person's cultural heritage. Muslims, for example, may not drink, and never eat pork.

Much of the business talk will go on during and after the meal rather than before, since this is the time to develop your relationship with small talk. Whoever has offered the invitation for the dinner or drinks is usually responsible for paying the bill, but it is important to reciprocate and not take anyone's hospitality for granted.

chapter nine

COMMUNICATING

LANGUAGE

While Sri Lanka is a trilingual nation, there are only two official languages—Sinhala and Tamil. Sinhala is spoken by around 74 percent of the population, most of whom are Sinhalese, while Tamil is spoken by around 25 percent. English is also widely spoken, and was the official language of Ceylon until shortly after independence. The Sri Lankan Creole Malay language is spoken in the homes of the Malay population.

Language is a controversial subject. The passing of the "Sinhala Only" law in 1956, demoting the Tamil language and thus excluding Tamils from taking up government positions, was one of the major underlying causes of the civil war. While Tamil was reinstated as an official language in 1988, the topic is still politically sensitive.

Sinhala is an Indo-Aryan language, spoken only in Sri Lanka. It evolved, influenced by successive waves of settlers and colonists, from the language Prince Vijaya and his entourage brought to the island in the fifth century BCE. Tamil, and to a lesser extent Portuguese, Dutch, Malay, and English have all contributed to it. Its closest linguistic relative is the Maldivian Dhivehi. While Sinhala is spoken island-wide, it has little

impact in the Tamil-dominated north and east. Written and colloquial Sinhala are not phonologically related, and the beautiful, curvilinear script is comprised of forty-seven characters.

Tamil is an ancient language spoken predominantly in southern India, as well as in Malaysia and Singapore. It belongs to the southern branch of the Dravidian language and was brought to Sri Lanka by South Indian invaders from the third century BCE. Sri Lankan Tamil is a distinct dialect, having over the years acquired its own accent and vocabulary, spoken widely in the north and east, and less so in

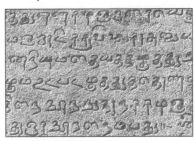

Colombo and the Hill Country. The Tamil script, while also curvilinear, is characterized more by rectangular shapes than the Sinhala script.

Sri Lankan English is unique, in that it has developed its own expressions, words, and idiosyncrasies of spelling, grammar, and punctuation. Since independence and its cessation as a national language, it has evolved to incorporate more Sinhalese vocabulary and grammatical conventions: for example, a "hotel" can mean a roadside restaurant, a "saloon" a hair salon, while "short eats" are snacks. The use of the tag word "no?" at the end of sentences such as "You're coming back, no?" and the frequent omission of the definite article (the) are typical characteristics of Sri Lankan English.

Muslims speak Tamil peppered with Arabic words, although those living in the south and west of the island may also speak Sinhala. English is typically the mother tongue of the Burghers, while it is the second language for many Sri Lankans living in cities and tourist areas. Westernized urbanites and better-educated Sinhala speakers often combine English words and phrases with their own language, curiously dipping in and out of both as they speak. All official signs, banknotes, and government papers, are printed in the three languages, while many businesses and shops have signs in Sinhala and English, Tamil and English, or all three, depending on their location.

While you can easily travel around Sri Lanka speaking only English, it is good idea to learn some Sinhala, as Sri Lankans will deeply appreciate your efforts at communication. It is easier to learn than Tamil, and you will encounter it more commonly on a daily basis. Many teachers of English offer private Sinhala language lessons to foreigners. Making mistakes is fine, and while some people may be amused when a foreigner speaks their language, you shouldn't be put off, since this usually just represents surprise. The next reaction will be to talk to you to find out how much you really know!

Sri Lankans often ask, "What to do?" when they are in an unfamiliar or uncomfortable situation. This can be a rhetorical question while they search for a possible solution, or can approximate to a Western shrug of the shoulders. It is also said in consolation, or in response to something where it is obvious that no solution can be given, and in these cases simply means, "Nothing can be done."

GESTURES AND BODY LANGUAGE

The most characteristic nonverbal form of communication in Sri Lanka is the famous head waggle. In conversation, someone will often signal assent, agreement, or understanding by moving the head from side to side, and at the same time slightly up and down, and saying "*Ha*." At first sight a foreigner might interpret this as shaking the head in disagreement, but on closer inspection it can be seen that the Sri Lankan action is in fact very different.

To beckon someone toward them, a Sri Lankan will hold one arm outstretched and, with the palm facing down, move the fingers inward. It is considered impolite to point at someone using the index finger, so gestures of moving the head or raising the eyebrows in the direction of the subject are commonly used. Hand gestures are often used to highlight a point.

Sri Lankans are less aware of personal distance than people in the West, so conversations between two friends are often carried out in very close proximity to each other. The opposite is true when a Sri Lankan is speaking to his superior, where the greater the social divide, the greater the personal distance maintained.

THE MEDIA

The Sri Lanka media is trilingual. Newspapers, television, and radio stations come in Sinhala, Tamil, and English, and are either state or privately owned. The extensive English-language media comprises a selection of dailies, including *The Island*, *Daily News*, *Daily Mirror*, and *The Nation*, as well as a few weekly newspapers such as the state-owned *Sunday Observer* and the privately run *Sunday Times*. Sinhala and Tamil newspapers are as numerous, and enjoy wide circulations in their homelands, reflecting the high literacy rate of the population. Newspapers are available from newsstands and independent retailers alongside a growing range of travel, lifestyle, and business-oriented magazines. Many newspapers have online editions.

The television channels broadcast almost entirely in Sinhala and Tamil, although there are some

English-language radio stations. Satellite television is becoming increasingly popular where foreign broadcasters such as the BBC, CNN, and Al-Jazeera offer an international perspective on events both in the country and worldwide.

There is no official censorship of the Sri Lankan media; however, there have been incidents in the past. There are guidelines discouraging negative reporting of the war, and in the light of an increasing number of assaults on journalists over the last few years, some privately owned newspapers and broadcasters have begun to exercise their own degree of self-censorship.

SERVICES
Telephone

The Sri Lankan telecommunications industry has seen extraordinary growth in the past decade. It is the most liberalized telecommunications industry in South Asia, and was one of the first in the region to launch 3G mobile phones. The installation of modern and efficient phone systems for both fixed and mobile connections means that calling anywhere in the world is easy. Communication bureaus offering IDD calls, fax, photocopying, and e-mail services are more popular than pay phones and can be found in almost every town and village. Calls are charged by the minute.

Sri Lankan cell phone networks are based on GSM and CDMA technology. Most UK, Australian, and New Zealand cell phones work well in Sri Lanka, although those from the USA that aren't tri-band might not. The five main cell phone networks are Dialog, Mobitel, Tigo, Hutch, and newcomer Airtel. Prepaid cards are available at nearly every communications bureau—look out for which company's sign and stickers emblazon the shop—and local SIM cards are cheap. If your cell phone does not accept foreign SIM cards, you can go to a phone shop and get it "unlocked" for a small fee.

Fixed telephone lines can be costly to install, and waiting lists are long. The state-run Sri Lanka Telecom has the majority market share.

Mail
While domestic mail in Sri Lanka is notoriously slow and erratic, airmail is usually very reliable. Since mail might be opened at customs, or lost or damaged in transit, it is a good idea to register it or send it by EMS Speed Post—a faster airmail service that takes three or four days to reach Europe and less than a week to reach the USA. International couriers FedEx and DHL both have offices in Colombo. Businesses in Colombo prefer to hand deliver important documents directly to their client's offices wherever possible.

Sri Lanka has a good network of post offices, reaching even the smallest rural villages. Money orders, payment of utility bills, and fines for automobile traffic offenses are other services handled at post offices. Mailmen deliver mail on foot, or by bicycle—tinkling their bell from the roadside outside a house to signal their arrival. Mailboxes on the streets are not always regularly emptied, so it is best to take your mail to a post office. If sending a package, you must take it unsealed, as the contents have to be checked.

Major post offices operate longer hours than smaller ones, and may be open from 7:00 a.m. to 9:00 p.m. during the week and all day Saturday.

When addressing mail, it is important to write the person's name, house number, street, village, and postcode, in that order. A full list of postcodes can be found on the Sri Lanka Post Web site (www.slpost.gov.lk). If sending mail to someone who is not a permanent resident at the address, always send it c/o the name of someone who is.

Internet

Internet access is widely available. There are communications bureaus thoughout the island and an increasing number of people have it at home. There are a few Internet Service Providers, the most popular of which is Sri Lanka Telecom (SLT), which offers broadband ADSL connections in most parts of the country for a flat monthly rate. While the average connection speed is 512 kbps, it is also possible to pay more for a faster connection speed of up to 2 mbps.

Wi-Fi has taken off in Sri Lanka. Many five-star hotels, shopping malls, and restaurants island-wide are now Dialog Wi-Fi hot spots.

CONCLUSION

Sri Lanka is a country of great contrasts and diversity, where the people are genuinely friendly, welcoming, and warm. Inequalities exist between the wealthy Westernized elite and the rural villagers, and there are discrepancies among the four major religions and the two main ethnic groups; what is shared, however, by all Sri Lankans is respect for family, home, and friendship, and pride in their beautiful island. They have shown great resilience in the face of the tsunami and the civil war.

Trust takes some time to earn, and although tempers may flare, they are easily and quickly calmed. Sri Lankans are characteristically indirect, but we know that this comes not from avoidance or discourtesy, but from a wish not to disappoint, cause embarrassment, or lose face. Politeness, respect, a genuine attempt to understand their culture, and acceptance of the island's relaxed pace, are the keys to gaining acceptance in turn by Sri Lankans and to having an enjoyable visit.

Further Reading

Amirthalingam, G. *Customs and Cultures of Sri Lanka*. London: A & S Books, 2003.

De Silva, K.M. *A History of Sri Lanka*. Colombo: Vijitha Yapa Publications, 2005.

Dissanayake, J.B. *Say it in Sinhala*. Colombo: Lake House Investments, 1993.

Gunaratne, Malinga H. *Tortured Island and the Price of Peace*. Ratmalana: Vishva Lekha, 2005.

Gunawardene, C.A. *Encyclopedia of Sri Lanka*. New Delhi: Sterling Publications, 2006.

Meyler, Michael. *A Dictionary of Sri Lankan English*. Colombo: Michael Meyler, 2007.

Tambiah, Stanley J. *Buddhism Betrayed? Religion, Politics and Violence in Sri Lanka*. Chicago: University of Chicago Press, 1992.

Thomas, Gavin. *The Rough Guide to Sri Lanka*. London: Rough Guides, 2006.

culture smart! **sri lanka**

Index

BT 3/09

Acknowledgments

For Buddika and my family with all my love. Thank you for your unending patience and support.